Youth in Transition
The Sociology of Youth and Youth Policy

Edited by
Claire Wallace and Malcolm Cross

Explorations in Sociology No. 37

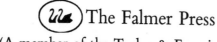 The Falmer Press
(A member of the Taylor & Francis Group)
London • New York • Philadelphia

UK   The Falmer Press, Rankine Road, Basingstoke, Hampshire
RG24 0PR

USA   The Falmer Press, Taylor & Francis Inc., 1900 Frost Road,
Suite 101, Bristol, PA 19007

First published 1990

British Library Cataloguing in Publication Data
Youth in transition: the sociology of youth and youth policy. —
    (Explorations in Sociology no. 37)
1. Great Britain. Youth
I. Wallace, Claire *1956*–   II. Cross, Malcolm   III. Series
305.230941.

ISBN 1-85000-797-7
ISBN 1-85000-798-5 pbk

Library of Congress Cataloging-in-Publication Data
Youth in transition: the sociology of youth and youth policy/edited
    by Claire Wallace and Malcolm Cross.
p.   cm.
        Includes bibliographical references.
        ISBN 1-85000-797-7 — ISBN 1-85000-798-5 (pbk.)
    1. Youth — Great Britain — Social conditions.   2. Youth —
    Great Britain — Economic conditions.   3. Occupational training
    — Great Britain.   4. Youth — Government policy — Great
    Britain.   I. Wallace, Claire.   II. Cross, Malcolm.
    HQ799.8.G7Y68
    305.23′ 5′ 0941—dc20

Jacket design by Caroline Archer

Typeset in 12/14 Bembo by
Chapterhouse, The Cloisters, Formby L37 3PX
Printed in Great Britain by
Taylor & Francis (Printers) Ltd, Basingstoke
*on paper which has a specified pH value on final paper manufacture of not
less than 7.5 and is therefore 'acid free'.*

Contents

Chapter 1

Introduction: Youth in Transition

Claire Wallace and Malcolm Cross

Ten years ago a book about the sociology of youth would have largely concentrated upon youth cultures and sub-cultures. The seminal work of the Centre for Contemporary Cultural Studies and others associated with it had identified 'youth' as a new and sociologically important area of study while at the same time denying that 'youth' itself was a 'real' social category (cf. Hall and Jefferson, 1977; Mungham and Pearson, 1976; Brake, 1980). This work had a number of common themes: the research was based on qualitative interviews, using an analytical framework derived from Marxist cultural studies and was focused on male youth in more exotic subcultures (Mods and Rockers, Skinheads, etc.). There were a number of criticisms made of this body of work including the exaggerated claims made for the significance of these trends and the poverty of the empirical work on which the studies were based.

Seen in the light of what has happened since, it is now clear that 'youth' were constructed as a social category in particular ways. The relative affluence of working-class youth — the majority of whom entered the labour market at 15 or later 16 — was distinctive when compared to either the pre-war situation or to their European counterparts. This led to youth being identified as consumer trend-setters and as a social avant-garde whose apparent flouting of conventions and anomic behaviour became a focus of public concern and cause for 'moral panic' (Cohen, 1972). From the sociologist's point of view what mattered were those groups at the cutting edge of change, for from them we could read off wider social and cultural developments. Indeed for some particular categories of young people, the claim has been made that they came to crystallize much that was wrong with Britain and had therefore a major political significance. John Solomos, for example, in a recent book on the way

1

in which black youth came to be defined, has claimed: '. . . many of the inputs which went into the racialisation of British political life were mediated via popular and policy concern about the "problem" of young blacks growing up in "ghetto environments"' (Solomos, 1988, p. 88). One of the responses to this was to argue for the extension of the Youth Service in order to attract young people off the streets and away from commercial (and allegedly frivolous) entertainment.

Since then the situation of young people has changed dramatically and so have the sociological paradigms used to study them. Unemployment has risen to levels undreamed of fifteen years ago and become an accepted fact of life. Young people are particularly affected by this. A range of policies have been developed to deal with the problem of young people who are unemployed and these have themselves served to construct a new model of youth and to redefine their status. For the first time in Britain, youth has become a category for large-scale policy intervention outside of education. There has been substantial sociological research into these trends, but most studies so far have concentrated upon jobs and the labour market, rather than other aspects of young people's lives — such as their housing situation or domestic life. Some might argue that this illustrates the way in which sociology has followed in the wake of economic trends and public policy, rather than being driven by its own theoretical imperatives. This is to some extent inevitable and one long standing and perfectly respectable role for sociology is to document the consequences of economic change and public policy interventions. The chapters in this volume reflect the change from studying youth as self-contained instigators of change to examining the role they have come to play as the unprecedented target of official attention.

It is important also to recognize the way in which methods and theories have shifted. The chapters in this book represent some of the leading trends in the field and many of them are based on large-scale survey investigation. Although some have recently argued that British sociology has been slow to respond to the statistical sophistication in the US, this is less true in the case of youth studies (cf. Bulmer, 1991). Contributions from the continuous survey run by the Centre for Educational Sociology in Edinburgh and by a number of researchers involved with the ESRC's 16–19 initiative mainly examine schooling experiences and transitions to training, unemployment and work with the aid of large-scale data sets. Thus a rich data base is being assembled for the study of young people in the 1980s and 1990s.

Unfortunately, this trend towards intensive and sophisticated data gathering is not yet matched by parallel developments in theory. The most interesting ideas relate to a new role for youth arising because of the interaction between young people and changes elsewhere in society. For example, the collapse of the labour market for the minimum age school-leaver has made young people more dependent on the family at a time when family bonds are themselves weakening. This creates tensions which earlier maturation previously did something to lessen. Similarly, increasing regional disparities in economic growth have forced some young people to leave home. However, the decline in real wages for young people and the massive pressure on housing have generated a major crisis of homelessness and poverty which is only too visible on the streets of London. The major line of theorizing, however, has been in relation to state intervention, and it is to policy issues that we now turn.

Developments in Youth Policy

Over the past fifteen years there have been a number of crucial developments in the situation of young people. First, rising youth unemployment led to a dramatic change in their opportunities and, as a consequence, a massive rise in the scale of policy intervention. Table 1:1 illustrates the scale of this change over the decade until 1986. Those in full-time education have risen from 40 per cent to 45 per cent with a tendency for more girls to stay on in education. The variety of educational courses provided by schools and colleges, including vocational and pre-vocational courses, Technical and Vocational Educational Initiatives (TVEI), Certificates in Pre-Vocational Education (CPVE), Business and Technical Qualifications (BTEC) and others has extended the choice for those not entering the labour market at the minimum age. Interestingly, these changes are seldom the result of initiatives taken by schools or colleges themselves. The running has been made by the 'new educators' who reside in the DES or the Training Agency. Taken with the advent of the National Curriculum and other changes in the 1988 Education Reform Act, we have witnessed a dramatic rise in external influence on education and an equally sudden demise of the power of teachers and local education authorities. The range on offer, combined with the external initiation of these new courses, has meant an apparent diversification of opportunities for young people

Table 1.1: Educational and economic activities of 16-year olds
Great Britain   *Percentages and thousands*

	1976[1]			1986[1]		
	Boys	Girls	Total	Boys	Girl	Total
Percentage of 16-year-olds who were[2]:						
In full-time education						
School	28	28	28	30	32	31
Further Education[3]	10	14	12	11	18	14
Total	38	42	40	41	50	45
In employment (outside YTS)[4]	54	51	53	15	16	15
On YTS/YOP[5]	—	—	—	31	24	27
Unemployed[6]	7	7	7	13	10	12
Total 16-year-olds (= 100%) (thousands)	420	401	821	441	419	860
of which in part-time day education (percentages)[7]	20	6	13	7	3	5

1. The activities in January each year of those who had attained the statutory school-leaving age (16 years) by previous 31 August.
2. In addition to the activities shown, some 10 per cent of 16-year-olds attend evening classes.
3. Full-time and sandwich including higher education, but excluding private education outside school. Excludes those on YTS in colleges.
4. Includes in 1976 and 1982 the unregistered unemployed and those who were neither employed nor seeking work (e.g. because of domestic responsibilities) and in 1986 those who are seeking work but not claiming benefit and those who are neither employed nor seeking work.
5. Includes those in further education establishments attending Youth Training Scheme/Youth Opportunities Programme courses.
6. Registered unemployed in 1976 and 1982 and claimant unemployed in 1985/86. (These are Department of Education and Science estimates.)
7. Public sector part-time study only (excluding those attending YTS courses). The majority are in employment, but some are receiving unemployment benefit.
Source: Department of Education and Science.
Source: Social Trends 18, 1988.

themselves, although the chapters which follow illustrate that patterns of post-school trajectory still follow traditional courses. The choice in practice is often between a YTS scheme or some sort of vocational college or school course. The tendency for many young people to stay on in school cannot necessarily be taken as evidence of a new found enthusiasm for education itself.

What is striking, however, is that the numbers going directly into employment have dropped dramatically from 53 per cent in 1976 to just 15 per cent in 1986, reflecting the virtual collapse of the youth labour market for 16- and 17-year-olds. Nearly one third of all school-leavers now enter a Youth

Training Scheme (YTS) and there has been a rise in youth unemployment from 7 per cent in 1976 to 12 per cent in 1986 which has impacted more forcibly on young men.

Schooling has traditionally entailed the twin objectives of personal discipline and the acquisition of knowledge. The same has been true in vocational training. It is striking, however, that faced with the rise in youth unemployment in the late 1970s, the former was perceived as being required by those who traditionally left school at 16. The Youth Opportunities Programme (YOP), which was introduced in 1977, focused on the most 'disadvantaged' young people and gave them a six month scheme which concentrated on 'life and social skills', remedial education and work experience. As unemployment continued to rise in the early 1980s, it became less and less tenable to tackle the problem as one of employability and the Youth Training Scheme was introduced in 1981 to supplement an attempt to instil work discipline with one designed to remedy skill shortage (Cross, 1987b). This provided a bridge with dual carriageways between school and work for all school-leavers. Reflecting as it did an implicit dual theory of training, it was no surprise to discover that those typically edged towards the inferior stream were ill-served by these developments (Cross, 1987b; Cross, 1988). The scheme was extended in 1986 to two years and was reinforced by the removal of entitlement to benefit and income support for those under 18. In this way, 100,000 16–18-year-olds were removed from the register in April 1988 (Stewart and Stewart, 1988).

These interventions substantially transformed the pathways into work and established a newly interventionist role by the state in relation to youth which some have argued amounts to an implicit 'national youth policy' (Davies, 1986). As well as being divided by social class, young people are now divided by their records of employment, unemployment, the kinds of schemes they have joined and their ways through the profusion of new educational qualifications. New models of youth and class are being devised to take this into account (Jones, 1987; and cf. Furlong in this volume). Some have argued that this gives rise to a process of 'individualization' whereby individuals need to map their own routes through a confusing array of opportunities and take increasing responsibility for the risk of failure in this process (Chisholm and Brown, 1990). Others have suggested, however, that this is simply the social reproduction of class, gender and ethnic relations in another form (Jones and Wallace, 1990). Certainly, YTS generates its own internal stratification

5

system, originally between Mode A (work experience with employers) and Mode B (special schemes for those deemed hard to employ) but more recently evident in the division between 'basic' and 'premium' funding of places (Cross, 1988). These schemes completely bypass the academic track and are intended for the educational low achievers who are the most vulnerable to rising unemployment.

Youth training is once more undergoing organizational change. At the time of writing the Youth Training Scheme is becoming simply 'Youth Training' (YT) and linked more closely to adult Employment Training. Funding and places are being cut in anticipation of a fall in youth unemployment in the 1990s as the demographic age-bulge works its way through. The use of the term 'YTS' throughout this volume represents the status of the scheme at the time research was carried out.

As a number of the early chapters in this book show, what has been provided through YTS is riddled with contradictions. David Lee and his colleagues are interested in developing a sociological account of YTS. They concentrate on developing the theoretical concepts of a 'surrogate labour market' and 'surrogate employment' in elucidating the paradox contained within YTS between the free market mechanism and massive state sponsored intervention.

Bob Coles and Robert MacDonald pursue an analogous concern. For them a key issue in the coming of YTS is its relationship to the 'Enterprise Culture'. On the one hand, YTS and its cousin Employment Training attempt to improve the national training picture and to promote standard and transportable qualifications. On the other hand, they have also incorporated training in 'enterprise' which, by its very nature, is locally and situationally specific. This tension suggests that national initiatives will be hard put to promote wholly new economic activity.

In looking in more detail at YTS in operation, Ken Parsons identifies the continuing salience of a contradiction that was contained in the early years of YOP. On the one hand, trainers were expected to provide a rounded experience for young people, particularly those who had not had an opportunity to develop the 'social and life skills' which were assumed to be missing in working-class culture. On the other, the market dictates that what is needed are skills determined by the needs of industry. The outcome is yet another tension with which the scheme is burdened.

A final tension in YTS is that between the economic climate which spawned it and that of the present. As unemployment falls so the need for the new vocationalism falters. As Joan Chandler suggests, one upshot of this is that national provision gives way in the face of increasing regional differences. On this basis YTS may fade away first in the South-east but remain a major linkage between school and work in the North. Moreover, a key issue in the analysis of what YTS has meant for the British economy is whether it has provided trainees with the capacity to compete effectively in the wider labour market beyond the firm in which they may have experienced their training or placement. David Raffe's data suggests a negative answer. Only a tiny proportion of 19-year-olds had gained their full-time jobs on the basis of skills acquired during their YTS training.

The coming of YTS has served to extend the period of 'youth' and has institutionalized it as an age-phase (Wallace, forthcoming). It has provided jobs for a new range of welfare professionals to guide, assess and monitor the progress of young people in different institutional environments. Consequently the idea of what 'youth' is needs to be revised. Rather than being setters of trends, they have become to some objects of pity and concern. Changes in social security and housing benefits, introduced as part of the review of social security from 1986 onwards, have made young people even more vulnerable and dependent. The rationale was to reduce the incomes of young people and to encourage training, but also to shift the onus of responsibility for those up to 18 firmly back to the family. Entitlement to income support was abolished for those under 18 and reduced for those under 25. Housing benefits were changed in such a way as to make it more difficult for young people to leave home while changes to the regulations governing Board and Lodgings payments mean that young people cannot stay in one place for more than a few weeks. These are being phased out altogether, starting in April 1989. Moreover, changes in the privately rented sector with the deregulation of rents and lower limits set on the payment of Housing Benefit particularly affect young people who are heavily dependent upon privately rented accommodation when they leave home. The advent of the poll tax will further reduce real incomes of young people over 18, since even the poorest will have to contribute at least 20 per cent of the individual rate. The Young Worker's Scheme and, after that, the New Worker's Scheme paid employers a subsidy for paying low wages in an attempt to reduce payments to the young. YTS allowances are also set very low and have not kept up with inflation in a further attempt to shift the burden of support. The results have been a dramatic fall in the standards of living of the young during the 1980s. This particularly affects working-class young people who traditionally have left school for work at the minimum age and made a contribution to family finances. Most middle-class young people would not have left education at 16 so the affect has been less, although the advent of the student loan scheme against furious opposition, together with the cutting of the real value of student grants, will generate greater dependence here too (Wallace, 1988).

The increased dependency of young people on the home may have resulted in a change to parent–child relations. More seriously, for those without a family to turn to the new pressures have had very dramatic consequences. It does not take sociology to record the evident increase in homelessness and destitution amongst the young. In 1985, it has been estimated that 85,000 young people were living on the streets. It is often argued that youth homelessness is a function of pressures on housing in overheated local economies. In analyzing the phenomenon in South Wales, Mark Liddiard and Susan Hutson show that problems of affordable accommodation and unemployment make young people vulnerable wherever they combine. These problems are exacerbated by policies specifically geared to relocate the responsibility for young people on to themselves or on to their families.

The relationship between this new phenomenon and the drugs trade, or crime in general, is one important area for further research. Youth has become a battleground for competing political ideologies. On the one hand, those who support the current measures see in them an attempt to counter the supposed breakdown of parental responsibility and thereby make a contribution to reducing juvenile crime, inner city riots and other acts of youthful deviance (Abbott and Wallace, 1989). Opponents would argue equally vehemently that standards of training have not risen, that career opportunities have been constrained rather than opened up and that problems of deviance have been exacerbated.

It is significant that whilst the changes of the last few years in Britain have been associated with the resurgence of a radical right wing philosophy, in Australia similar legislation has been introduced by a government of the political centre, the consequences of which are discussed by Mike Presdee. This may suggest a redefinition of youth in capitalist societies more generally, possibly associated with the perceived need to extend education and training in line with new technology. In this regard much of the running is being made by

West Germany and Japan who appear to be putting so many more resources into vocational education and training.

It is important to note, however, that these developments are not uniformly felt by all young people. Young women are still likely to receive education and training which equips them for low status, low paid, 'feminized' occupations (Cockburn, 1987). Andy Furlong shows that old correlations between social class and educational qualifications remain over the decade of his study. In particular the likelihood of long term unemployment was powerfully correlated with poor educational attainment. Similarly, Afro-Caribbean young people are more likely than others to go on training schemes but these tend to be of a kind that will be less likely to equip them with relevant skills. Asian young people, by contrast, are much more likely than their peers to stay on in school or college rather than risk this uncertain transition into work (Cross, Wrench and Barnett, 1990). Furthermore, there are important regional differences, partly as a result of different policies pursued by individual local authorities. In Sheffield, for example, which is the administrative home of the Training Agency, the City has taken over much of the training provision, while in Liverpool the local authority would have little to do with YTS. The nature of the local labour market varies considerably between localities, providing quite different opportunities for young people who are largely dependent upon localized amenities.

In assessing the relative merits of youth training when compared with staying on in education, albeit with a greater vocational content, little attention is paid to the additional benefits of the latter in providing socialization into the productive use of leisure time. Ken Roberts and his co-authors show that an unintended consequence of youth training is the re-establishing of class and gender differences in the experience of leisure. In this sense educational provision beyond the age of 16, whether accompanied by additional qualifications or not, may make important contributions to the quality of life.

At the dawn of the 1990s, unemployment is falling and the number of young people available to enter the labour force has been reduced as a result of smaller age cohorts. This increases the demand for young people and threatens to make YTS once again a residual scheme for the unemployed. The pressure is on to make employers shoulder more of the costs of vocational training and the White Paper of 1988(b) presages the end of the 'training culture' of the past decade and the return to *laissez-faire*. The demise of the Manpower Services

Commission is also symptomatic of this change.

What is left is a plethora of new vocational qualifications and a trend towards increasing certification. Whereas 21 per cent of young people left school with no qualifications in 1975/76 only 9 per cent did so in 1986 (Social Trends, 1989). The implementation of the 1988 Education Reform Act in April 1990 further institutionalizes a vocational bias as school governors have by law to include representatives of business and commerce. The Secretary of State for Education has gained for himself more than 400 new powers, including that of founding brand new City Technology Colleges in selected urban areas. The question is whether we revert to the old system, which fostered low skill levels and twin-track entry to the labour market, or whether the culmination of all these changes will increase opportunities and raise standards. The essays in this volume suggest that race, gender, social class and locality are still likely to be highly significant determinants of what it it like to be young in the 1990s.

Chapter 2

Surrogate Employment, Surrogate Labour Markets and the Development of Training Policies in the Eighties

David J. Lee
(with Dennis Marsden, Penny Rickman and Jean Duncombe)

There is rarely a simple correspondence between politicians' assumptions about labour markets and the way these markets work in practice. A topical example is the so-called free market approach to social policy. This seeks to achieve welfare objectives by encouraging the calculative pursuit of individual market advantage rather than through intervention and legislation. In practice the behaviour of labour market participants is more complex than the dogma suggests and what is rational for individuals is often irrelevant to the policy as a whole (e.g. Dombois, 1989). Also, it is virtually impossible in practice for policies to be either purely free market, or, as state socialist economies have found, purely interventionist. Sociologists can help to raise the level of political discussion by means of comparative research, looking at how the balance between intervention and market forces varies between particular initiatives and programmes and what this means for the outcome in each case.

This paper offers some theoretical ideas for developing a comparative study of programmes of training and work experience adopted in Europe and America in recent years. Recession and technological uncertainties have threatened most Western societies with a labour market crisis of redundant skills and rapidly shifting employment patterns. We shall argue that the stock response of governments to the problem, despite wide variations in political creeds, may usefully be conceptualized by the related notions of 'surrogate employment' and 'surrogate labour market' (SLM). We begin by defining these terms and illustrating briefly their validity across a range of superficially different programmes. We then consider a major example, the Youth Training

Scheme (YTS) developed by the British Government since 1983. Developing the conclusions of a five year study of YTS in one town in south-east England, we explore the supply and demand for the labour of school-leavers which the Scheme created. We argue that our approach makes it possible to explain why many features of the Scheme have been self defeating.

Surrogate Employment and Surrogate Labour Markets

Surrogate employment is *work created or regulated by legislative or administrative intervention with the declared aim of remedying deficiencies in the quantity and/or quality of demand for labour.* Typically, the workers affected do not have regular contracts of employment in the accepted sense though the conditions under which they work for employers may be fixed through a training agreement or similar document. Surrogate employment always involves a variable balance of power between the centralizing and standardizing effects of intervention and the centrifugal influence of 'market forces'. In practice, the rational self interest of employers and workers often induces them to manipulate the terms and rules of the programme. A principal task of empirical research is to explain the range of variation in outcomes which according to the rules ought to be uniform.

A surrogate labour market is *any network of work placements which exists alongside or additional to conventional contractual employment.* On one hand the state attempts to bring about a condition (e.g. more employment, a more work oriented youth labour force, better training, an increased supply of skilled labour) which the unaided market has manifestly failed to provide. On the other hand it pursues these aims by affecting the commercial behaviour of employers through subsidies and legislation, and the self interest of workers through grants and benefits contingent on observing the rules of the programme. (The limiting case occurs where the state itself becomes the surrogate employer — but even here the influence of market forces is to be found.) Surrogate labour markets can be analyzed through the conceptual apparatus used for labour markets in general. The impact of intervention on employers can be treated as a problem in the 'demand' for surrogate labour, while the impact on workers is a question of 'supply'. We shall argue too that surrogate employment, like normal employment, is liable to segmentation which is usually linked to imperfections in the 'real' labour market.

An obvious example of surrogate employment is found within so-called 'workfare' programmes in which welfare claimants must work in unpaid jobs in order to receive benefit payments. For serious analysis, however, the term 'workfare' by itself is vague and unhelpful. Even in the USA where the idea originated, it is applied to a range of schemes which vary greatly in extent and in the level of state administrative involvement and funding. Some schemes are confined to the 'job search' and 'job club' type of programme, leaving the provision of actual job *openings* wholly to the state of the local economy. Strictly speaking workfare must logically entail the *creation* of surrogate work where none is available on the open market. But there is much controversy in individual states over the extent of intervention and funding necessary to create work openings (Kosterlitz, 1985). Consequently, the surrogate 'work' element varies greatly in quality, according to whether or not the jobs are externally created, subsidized and monitored so as to provide recipients with the work experience necessary for them to become self sufficient, as the political philosophy of workfare requires. For example the Californian programme was criticized because work preparation assignments involved 'mopping floors, picking up litter in city parks and other menial activities' (Burghes, 1987, p. 11). In contrast the work programme in Massachusetts provided both training and support services for trainees and 'attracted more than 6,000 businesses to participate, from high tech manufacturers to small retail stores' (*ibid.*, pp. 16–17). On the 'supply' side too, the nature and powers of administrative intervention vary both in theory and in practice giving rise to questions such as who precisely comes within the scope of the scheme, how the rules are to be enforced and the behaviour of participants 'policed'. Thus the concept of a surrogate labour market highlights a number of unresolved dilemmas in the operation of the workfare principle, which perhaps explains why the system has not been as extensively taken up as is widely believed.

All of these American schemes contrast markedly with 'workfare' in Sweden where the Swedish Employment Service has a comprehensive responsibility for labour market policy measures, including finding employment or training for unemployed young people over 18 and the provision of relief jobs as a last resort against unemployment. In addition municipal authorities must arrange jobs on youth teams for young people who cannot be given work or training. This legal obligation to create surrogate employment requires considerable use of public funds to guarantee that social insurance is based on the 'employment principle' rather than the 'cash assistance principle' of the British post-war welfare state. Even so, the dilemmas inherent in creating employment alongside the 'real' labour market are not absent. For example, surrogate employment on this scale affects the supply of labour to the real labour market in depressed areas (Burton, 1987, p. 22). A common problem in both Swedish and American schemes, too, is that of 'creaming': jobs in work creation programmes are uneven in quality and the best openings go to those who least need the help they offer. As we shall see below 'creaming' is a very common problem of surrogate employment and can be found in YTS.

Of course, examples of surrogate labour markets can be found outside of so-called workfare programmes. In Europe, the deteriorating labour market conditions of the late seventies and early eighties forced many governments to adopt a range of work creation, retraining and unemployment programmes in which various combinations of administrative intervention and public subsidy were used to stimulate work placements with individual employers. Specific labour market measures used by the French Government, for example, included exempting firms from social security contributions, so encouraging them to increase their workforces and take on jobless youngsters. Practical in-firm training courses were introduced, lasting between six and eight months (CEDEFOP, Vol. 2, 1983). After 1981 job creation was targetted on public employment and labour intensive small and medium sized firms. Suggestions that the non-standard contracts of young people were being exploited by firms, however, led to the 'Youth Future Plan'. This offered 'employment training' contracts which could become a fixed secure job contract, though for a strictly defined period. In all of these initiatives the Government has actually increased the level of legally backed supervision over the commercial self interest of work providers in order to prevent abuses and to mesh with the state managed system of college based preliminary vocational training. Nevertheless, the inefficient provision of state subsidies gave rise to problems and abuses. Furthermore, one-sided state control was criticized as too rigid, bureaucratic, poorly coordinated and insufficiently responsive to changing needs of employment (*ibid.*, pp. 57–9). Public sector vocational training as a whole in France has been accused of being generally less effective in promoting economic growth than the German system (Maurice *et al.*, 1986).

In Germany, though job creation programmes also exist, *most* school leavers, and not just 'problem' groups, enter a surrogate labour market because of the celebrated 'dual' system of employer based apprenticeship. Apprentices do not have an employment contract and are paid an 'educational allowance' by their employers which is low relative to youth *wages* in other industrial societies. The training allowance and all other training costs have to be borne by the employer. But firms are only permitted to engage apprentices and undertake training under conditions closely regulated formally by law and informally by unions and works councils (Streek *et al.*, 1987). This must include attendance for part of the week at *Berufschule*.

Although the system is frequently praised (e.g. Wagner, 1986), it has a number of problematic features which again show the uneasy relationship between administrative regulation and commercial interest characteristic of surrogate employment in general. Even in the early seventies, when larger firms accounted for a higher proportion of places than today, there was considerable dissatisfaction among apprentices and their parents, and pressure to reduce the employers' role and expand the school based component of occupational preparation. Complaints were made that in practice training standards were very variable and that many employers, especially small firms, were able to flout their legal obligations (Reubens, 1973), in effect using apprentices as cheap labour. 'Creaming' was rife. Too many apprenticeable trades were receiving recognition. Training was too often dominated by increasingly obsolete traditional crafts. On completing their apprenticeship many young men were unable to enter the occupation for which they had been trained. The system had done little at all for young women. The 'untrammelled power of employers' was blamed for these faults (Reubens, 1973, p. 15).

Further problems emerged with the recession. Large firms began to cut their training activities back in order to save costs so creating a potential crisis of insufficient places at a time of rising youth unemployment. Yet in fact Germany subsequently appeared to be virtually the only industrialized country to meet the recession with a 'countercyclical' expansion of training places. This is partly explained by the fact that employer groups were threatened by the prospect of more state intervention, of losing their control over the regulation of training syllabuses and by the possible imposition of a training tax. Even so, numbers in training were only maintained by adding to the proportion of places in small firms and offices, precisely the type of 'apprenticeship' which already had been much criticized. Marginal firms have used vulnerable groups of young people as cheap labour, often substituting them for adult workers in order to survive adverse trading conditions (Casey, 1986). A recent study concluded that the transition to work has become more risky for young apprentices with fewer getting a good start in working life or able to enter jobs for which they had been trained. Apprenticeship was reflecting the divisions in the wider labour market between fully qualified work and peripheral employment (Herget, 1986). Thus, many of the supposedly unique qualities of the German 'dual system' appear to be less important sociologically than the characteristics it has *in common* with other surrogate labour markets.

We shall now describe how the idea of demand and supply in a surrogate labour market can be used as a framework for research on the impact of a particular programme. We draw here upon our own research on the Youth Training Scheme (YTS) in the UK but the main purpose of the discussion is theoretical rather than empirical and is intended to build on our previous work (Lee *et al.*, 1990).

YTS and the Demand for Surrogate Labour

As is well known, the origin of YTS closely parallels experience elsewhere. It was a response by the Government to rapidly growing youth unemployment and a recession-induced crisis in apprenticeship and other voluntarily provided employer based training. Employers supported it because they feared the Government would have to intervene more directly in their affairs if they did not participate (Keep, 1986).

Yet YTS became distinctive (and highly controversial) for three reasons. First, the Scheme was set up so as to reflect the Government's free market ideology and in particular a belief that training was best given in real work situations by employers exposed to market forces. The result was a highly decentralized structure, in which training is delegated to a plethora of so-called 'managing agents', mostly employers who volunteered training programmes for jobless youngsters within their own establishments. In addition specialist training organizations became managing agents of so-called 'umbrella' YTS schemes, delegating workplace training to a network of 'workproviders', mostly firms too small to be managing agents in their own right. This employer and market-led structure was intended to bear the main weight of provision. Only for the very severely disadvantaged and in extreme cases of market failure, notably in high unemployment localities where local industry had collapsed, was the more expensive option of publicly provided YTS training tolerated. The level of funding for these 'premium' (formerly Mode B) YTS places has gradually been cut. Free market dogma also shaped the legitimation and goals of the Scheme. Unemployment among young people, even if they were disadvantaged by gender, ethnicity or background, was said to be caused by their lack of marketable skills. Encouraging individual firms to train them in the scarce transferable skills most needed in the workplace would therefore improve their general employability. Thus, YTS also sought a free market solution to longstanding problems of socially disadvantaged youth.

But secondly, despite the free market rhetoric, considerable state expenditure and public intervention were needed to create 'real work situations' in the first place because the market had already demonstrably failed to do so. Employers had to be persuaded to offer placements. These were limited at first to one year of work experience and only later (1986) extended to two. Moreoever, YTS trainees have a training agreement, not a regular employment contract. However, firms could also bring their own trainee intake within the scheme and either have them paid the training allowance or offer them so-called employed YTS status from the outset. Administrative supervision of YTS training and control over standards was made the responsibility of a Government agency, the Manpower Services Commission (now absorbed into the Department of Employment and renamed the Training Agency (MSC/TA)). MSC gave the impression of a highly interventionist structure (Turbin, 1988), handing out 'state controlled training franchises' (Chandler and Wallace, 1989). The designers of the new scheme proclaimed it as a new beginning for Britain's young workers.

Yet in fact, MSC's interventions were still within the British 'pragmatic tradition of voluntarism in state–industry relations' (Sheldrake and Vickerstaff, 1987). This tradition always treated industrial training as wholly the responsibility of 'industry', not the state. Training was provided only where it was in firms' commercial self interest, so that the national budget of different types of skills and training was never planned or known in advance. YTS departed from this tradition only by setting up a surrogate labour market for trainees, using a subsidy to encourage employers to provide extra training places for unemployed youngsters. Nevertheless, the take up of the subsidy and the relation between a firm's regular training and YTS was left entirely to voluntary initiative. Furthermore, MSC's actual powers, even at their peak, were based merely on its ability to approve individual YTS schemes, agents and work providers for subsidy. Employers successfully resisted the principle of the German system, where workshop training is externally monitored and credentialled (Keep, 1986). And in recent years the subsidy element in YTS has been much reduced, and employers themselves are bearing a higher proportion both of the cost and the responsibility for running and moderating YTS. Thus, the surrogate labour market established by YTS was one in which the role of intervention was relatively superficial, with the balance of power between administrators and market forces tipped decisively in favour of the latter.

The third distinctive feature of YTS has been the speed and scale on which it expanded. This was dictated by the relatively large size of the UK's youth unemployment problems in the eighties and the urgency with which the Government wished to be seen to be tackling it. By 1986 nearly half of all 16-year-old leavers were on YTS. As we shall see the rapid growth further eroded MSC's scope for *dirigisme*.

Consequently, the scheme failed to achieve the objectives for which it was supposedly established. There is a persistent shortage of YTS training in shortage skills and an excess of YTS places in skills not in short supply (Deakin and Pratten, 1987; Ashton *et al.*, 1990). And despite the Government's declared hopes of making YTS the norm for all young people, employed and unemployed, it has remained mostly a job creation package.

Furthermore, opportunities within YTS are very uneven in quality. In our fieldwork, we found the YTS surrogate labour market fell into a pattern of labour market segmentation which once established greatly contributed to the policy's failure. To describe this it will be useful to distinguish (a) segmentation due to differentiation of participants before they enter the labour market and (b) differences between them caused by the operation of the market itself. This is usually referred to as the contrast between pre-market and in-market segmentation (e.g. Ryan, 1981).

Pre-market Segmentation of Labour Demand in YTS

This is largely the result of the origin of schemes, and in particular the impact of the subsidy on the financial calculations of employers of different kinds. Those with high training costs tended to be large manufacturing firms with established training facilities which often had been cut back because of the recession. Such organizations have tended to use the subsidy element in YTS only for their own training, merging their apprenticeship and training programmes into the Scheme. But the amount of new training of this kind was restricted because the subsidy was simply not high enough. Also large firms were quite often under union pressure to offer fully employed status to YTS trainees, or to top up the government training allowance from the outset, so adding further to costs. So firms with high training costs restricted their involvement with YTS and some did not participate at all, preferring to remain independent of the MSC/TA, especially if the administrative costs and workload of getting and retaining approval became excessive. Large firm training in costly transferable skills has thus tended to form a relatively small and exclusive 'top' layer in YTS.

At best, YTS stimulated some large firms to reopen training capacity which they had closed down during the recession so making extra places available. However the skills offered, for example in certain engineering crafts, could be ones for which the recession had reduced demand and did not necessarily lead trainees into a job at the end of their training (Turbin, 1988).

In addition, YTS schemes were developed from earlier training on the 'umbrella' pattern (see page 16). This relatively 'stable' type of YTS was derived from the activities of the old statutory Training Boards now being run down by the Government; or from former Group Training Associations run by consotria of small firms; or, finally trading associations. Like large employers, these organizations also tended, at least at the outset, to restrict their recruitment, largely because they too had a recognizable skill or standard of training which they were formally committed to defend and which entailed costs and time for training beyond the YTS subsidy. Examples in our study included schemes run by (or for) CITB, EITB, the Hairdressers' Federation and the local Chamber of Commerce.

The shortfall of YTS places in large firms and established training situations, however, led MSC to encourage the setting up of schemes in 'new skills' attached to occupations where little training tradition had been previously established. Although initially welcomed by some observers, the nature and scope of this 'new' training has threatened the original aim of YTS to provide quality training in skills which would increase the employability of young people. In most areas MSC/TA has had little information from which to plan the distribution of places in relation to local skill needs. Furthermore, the youth employment position in the early eighties created pressure to find as many YTS places as possible. So the MSC found itself bargaining and even pleading with all comers to make sufficient places available.

The new skill training schemes tended to be in occupations, largely but not exclusively in the services sector, where training costs (and typical skill levels) were low in relation to the size of the subsidy from YTS. Employers could reap a direct production benefit by substituting YTS trainees for adult fully waged workers. Furthermore, a variety of training entrepreneurs could make a living from organizing YTS training on an 'umbrella' basis. In our study local MSC staff found themselves negotiating and bargaining with a heterogeneous range of individuals and organizations, in order to meet their quotas of training places. Much of this entrepreneurial training was attached to small service sector organizations expanding rapidly with the consumer boom of the South-east.

Thus the differing origins of schemes resulted in a premarket segmentation of demand for YTS trainees which already ran counter to government claims that uniform standards of quality existed throughout YTS. We even found that schemes of varying quality were being offered to school leavers under the *same* skill labels.

In-market Segmentation

This affected YTS schemes as soon as they began to recruit, leading to variation in what Raffe (1986) has called *the recruitment context*. In effect, 'recruitment context' denotes the self-fulfilling prophecy linking employers' expectations of trainees at recruitment to their subsequent *chances of a job* with that employer at the end of the training. YTS as a whole suffers from this problem. The Government simultaneously tried to establish YTS as a viable alternative to extended schooling for all young people but also used it to absorb large numbers of young unemployed who typically are relatively poorly qualified and socially disadvantaged. So in practice it did not successfully overcome the 'low status' image which it inherited from its predecessor, the Youth Opportunities Programme and well qualified young people continued to avoid it. Likewise, employers' widespread belief that candidates for YTS places were of poor quality created a vicious circle of expectations which kept the number of places with good job prospects small.

Because of the widely varying origin of schemes, however, there is within YTS itself marked variation in the context from which the managing agents of individual YTS schemes recruit trainees and in the attractiveness of their typical work placements. The result is the phenomenon referred to earlier as 'creaming'. Large and stable firms and schemes attracted a surfeit of school leavers from which the most qualified could be recruited. These mostly performed as expected and so tended to get job offers later. But the smaller and less well known the site of the placement, the greater the difficulty the managing agent (or the employer or the Careers Service) had in 'selling' their training to potential trainees. The placements were typically the most precarious in the non-established entrepreneurial schemes and Mode B or premium schemes. They attracted only the least employable school leavers many with personal and social problems. Employers, some of whom openly admitted to exploiting the trainees, put them on probation to 'work themselves into a job'. Frequently they found themselves disappointed at the trainees' response to the 'chance' they had been given. So a vicious circle of insecurity for both sides built up.

These inequalities at the recruitment stage were reinforced by variation in *control over the content of training* between placements even within the same scheme. As we explained above, the MSC/TA had the responsibility of setting standards in particular areas of occupational competence and ensuring that they were adhered to. But as we have seen its main sanctions were its ability to withold its approval and subsidy of schemes and this lessened over time. Because MSC/TA's powers to control workplace training were limited, the independence of the training process from production pressures was under threat in all areas of YTS. Even in large concerns, line management would prioritize their need for the trainees' labour to meet deadlines and busy periods, against the demands of the training schedule agreed with MSC. Training officers had to assert their authority and did not always win the struggle. But the problem was much worse for umbrella schemes especially entrepreneurial schemes in non-established skills or covering many small firms and outlets.

Figure 2.1 charts rather crudely the broad pattern of segmentation of demand for surrogate labour under YTS. The columns represent in effect both the pre-market segmentation of schemes by origin and the closely related in-market segmentation of schemes and placements by their recruitment contexts. Both are reflected in the self-fulfilling relationship between, on the one hand, positive and negative 'creaming' and, on the other, typical job

Figure 2. 1: Segmentation and inequality of demand in the YTS surrogate labour market

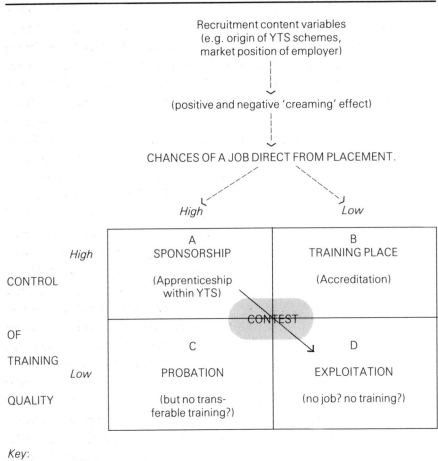

Key:
---> = causal link
———> = expected trend over time

chances associated with individual YTS schemes. The rows represent in-market segmentation caused by varying control over the training process in individual placements. The result is a loose classification of segments, though the reader should keep in mind the pervasive effects of gender which mean that the relative size of the categories differs for female and male labour market participants.

The classification overlaps with an earlier study of YTS *outcomes* by Raffe (1987b) but tries to model the factors which *cause* demand for surrogate labour to be segmented. Box A combines good quality training with good job chances and a selective intake. This is the elite sector of YTS which increasingly resembles employment under a normal contract. In Box B good training does not lead to a job within the placement. This is the credentialling sector of YTS which the Government hoped to expand so as to increase the supply of workers in the economy with transferable skills. In fact, survey evidence has tended to confirm our own conclusion that this sector is small and shrinking because the logic of the surrogate labour market outweighs the limited intervention through subsidy to expand good quality training (Raffe, 1987b, 1990), Boxes C and D represent deviant placements from the point of view of YTS. Box C shows that expanding training in non-established areas put trainees up on probation in terms of personal qualities motivation, and, at best, firm-specific skills. Box D represents the cheap labour function of YTS which is not officially admitted but which definitely corresponds to certain types of pressure within the YTS youth labour market. However, it should be noted that in our research an element of insecurity over prospects was felt by all but the most privileged trainees in YTS. We have reflected this by including a shaded segment of what Raffe calls 'contest' traineeship which overlaps all segments of the diagram. As some authors have suggested, these pressures may stem from the growth of flexible employment practices during the restructuring of the international labour market of the eighties (Pollert, 1986; Ashton *et al.*, 1990). Because of this restructuring we would also place most premium or Mode B traineeships within Box D despite the commitment which many individual trainers have to 'premium' young people in this sector and the good schemes which often exist there. However, as Chandler (1989) has shown, where a high proportion of youngsters are in premium YTS it is the poor job chances in the local labour market as a whole which leads to exploitation. In Chandler's study managing agents of premium schemes were adopting an increasingly managerial stance and using the trainees as a low cost labour force that bears disturbing parallels with the 'enterprise zones' of the Third World.

One further feature of Figure 2.1 is the diagonal arrow. This represents our original prediction that *ceteris paribus* the long term logic of demand in the surrogate labour market was to diminish the relative importance of all except the more exploitative sectors. But we were to find later that as the subsidy element in YTS was reduced this segment of YTS faced the prospect of severe contraction again. Indeed, the revival of real jobs for young people combined with the decline in the age group posed a severe 'marketing' problem for YTS as a whole in most relatively prosperous areas.

YTS and the Supply of Surrogate Labour

Pre-market segmentation on the supply side of any labour market

> is closely related to stratification. Some individuals enter the labour market with distinct advantages in terms of the knowledge, skills and attitudes conducive to success. Such capabilities contain a large developmental component, associated primarily with the family and the school, access to which is markedly differentiated according to . . . social class, race and sex. (Ryan, 1981: p. 4).

In the youth labour market, of course, the 'developmental component' is still interacting with the influences of the market itself. Also, relatively advantaged young people do not enter the labour market at all but continue in full time education often until early adulthood.

In the YTS surrogate labour market several such pre-market influences are evident, the major ones being gender, race, school attainment and family background. Our findings were wholly consistent with earlier research showing that despite YTS's commitment to 'equal opportunities' young women and black youth, unless exceptionally qualified, suffered market discrimination in access to the more skilled occupations, schemes and placements (e.g., Cockburn, 1987; Finn, 1987). But having allowed for ascriptive differences, school attainment is the most clearly important 'pre-market' difference between recruits to YTS. As we noted above, YTS suffers from 'creaming' because the elite schemes are able to be academically selective and exclude those most in need of the best training. At the other extreme youngsters recruited to the more dubious entrepreneurial schemes and Mode B/premium YTS, especially in occupations and firms with little training tradition, were only patchily qualified. True, for girls there are fewer unambiguously 'sponsored' YTS places to begin with. A high proportion of female placements are in fact contained within just three occupational areas, clerical, retailing and so-called 'care' occupations. However, the first appears to be the most academically selective — in our study about three fifths of female clerical trainees had at least one O level.

Social selection undoubtedly exists in YTS, too, but varies between schemes in subtle ways too complex to discuss here. Because brighter middle class youngsters are 'creamed off' to full time education or jobs, academic selectivity in elite YTS schemes tends to benefit the more able working class school leavers, boys especially. However our fieldwork indicated that middle class girls had an advantage in selection to clerical work even when less well qualified. In general however it was difficult to identify any uniform effects of social class not related to differences in educational achievement. We also found that the position is further complicated by the fact that well qualified and middle class 'prodigals' were often able to return to their class and educational roots after YTS, making good use of them even though YTS had been a disastrous experience. For the initially disadvantaged, however, a poor YTS actually worsened their chances.

A further complication was the independent influence of family and neighbourhood contacts. These are especially important in some industries like construction with a large number of small personally-owned businesses. Among boys particularly we found YTS being used to transmit small business ownership and job contacts from fathers to sons. But undoubtedly, across the spectrum of educational and social background family influence could confer an independent advantage.

We turn now to in-market segmentation of the labour supply. In order to understand how the YTS surrogate labour market itself creates and reinforces unequal opportunities we found it helpful to draw certain analogies between the workers in all surrogate labour markets and the inmates of total institutions (Goffman, 1968). Like the latter, the workers are deemed to be in need of some 'treatment' (skills training, more work experience, better motivation and self-presentation) before they can expect a normal job contract. Consequently, like inmates the trainees have a 'moral career', shaped by the interaction between their actual circumstances, especially the quality of the placement, and their self-perceptions. Some of these careers fit the official stereotype of the treatment and others are deviant. The result is further segmentation of workers' characteristics caused by surrogate employment itself.

As with in-market segmentation of the demand side of YTS, the calibre of the actual placement in terms of the quality of the training and the chances of a job afterwards are crucial. However, in relation to trainees' moral careers what matters is their *perceptions* of their situation as favourable or unfavourable, a factor which depends on a sense of how far a marketable skill has been learned, whether employers make promises of a job early in the training or defer their decision, the perceived prestige of the scheme, etc. Arguably, these perceptions contain an element of a self fulfilling prophecy reinforcing trainees' self identification as marketable or unmarketable. We especially noted the further decline in self image which some initially poorly qualified female trainees experienced under YTS, leading them to retreat into domesticity and motherhood.

Because the lives of young people are affected by a multitude of factors we were not able to identify clear groups of trainees with different 'moral careers'. But a somewhat crude classification, based on our findings, is presented in Figure 2.2 to show the outcomes which are theoretically possible and also useful in interpreting actual case histories. Again the figure presents the interaction of pre-market and in-market influences. The rows represent favourable and unfavourable pre-market factors and the columns represent favourable and unfavourable perceptions by trainees of their job chances. This gives four boxes corresponding to four main types of moral career which are theoretically possible.

In Box A highly selected trainees (protégés) typically performed as predicted, so reinforcing the prestige of the scheme. In Box B trainees disadvantaged by their pre-market background (and related joblessness)

Figure 2.2: Segmentation and inequality of supply in the YTS surrogate labour market

Pre-market segmentation: Primarily through school attainment

In-Market segmentation	High	Low
	A	C
LEARNING *Favourable*	PROTÉGÉS	TUTELAGE
AND	(Apprenticeship within YTS)	(Accreditation)
JOB	B	D
CHANCES *Poor*	MORAL RESCUE	DETACHMENT
	(Job(?) but no transferable training)	(exploitation)

perform above expectation and so experience what we have called 'moral rescue' through YTS. These two boxes fulfil the claims of the Government's publicity. In Box C trainees from a favourable background experience the YTS placement as poor relative to their expectation or fail to perform as expected but may be able to retrieve the situation by using prior background or qualifications gained on YTS. Box D represents a situation which is wholly deviant from the point of view of YTS in which disadvantaged trainees come up against a set of negative experiences during training and become 'detached' and alienated. The diagonal arrow again represents a prediction that over time the logic of the surrogate labour market will cause Box D cases to constitute an increasingly large proportion of the total. This is because well qualified young people have not been recruited to YTS in large numbers and the number of places in the elite sector of YTS has tended to regress to being normal employment with a job contract. Also, cases represented by Boxes B and C are less common.

Conclusions

The concepts of surrogate employment and a surrogate labour market have been used in this chapter to uncover a set of common dilemmas in a number of superficially unrelated training and job creation schemes. The central issue, we have argued, is where the balance of power should lie in the mix of administrative intervention and market forces which is virtually inevitable in such programmes. This gives rise to conflicts between individual and the public interest and between the enforcement of uniform standards and flexibility in the face of changing labour force needs. Since the basic dilemma is probably insoluble in any final sense, political debate should be about what direction a specific policy should move in at any given time rather than about the respective merits of 'interventionist' or 'free market' political philosophies in the abstract.

British experience, both under YTS and under the voluntaristic industrial training which preceded it, indicates that the labour market failure cannot be retrieved solely by market mechanisms themselves. A minimum requirement for the success of YTS would have been that the training, as in Germany, should be externally controlled and validated so as to enhance the prestige of the YTS trainees and their certificates. It follows that the most significant weakness of current youth training policy, which is now replacing YTS with an even more decentralized, employer led and funded system, is that it is moving in the wrong direction altogether and threatens to undermine the little that is left of externally controlled standards to say nothing of planned skill inputs into the economy.

Finally, British youth training under YTS has shared a problem with other forms of surrogate employment in that it has become linked to the marginal sectors of employment which arguably have expanded during the recession and uncertainty of the eighties. Our analysis supports those who argue that this form of state intervention has actually helped (and even sought) to create a flexible labour force of government trainees and workfare claimants. But it also shows that the more basic problem is the vicious circle joining the intervention to market forces. It was the failure of the market which precipitated the intervention but in turn the intervention creates a new source of social and economic stigma for the (mostly already disadvantaged) workers who are caught up by it. Thus the most pressing political issue is how a vicious circle can be turned into a virtuous one.

Chapter 3

From New Vocationalism to the Culture of Enterprise

Bob Coles and Robert F. MacDonald

This chapter reviews the activities of the Manpower Services Commission (MSC) and the Training Agency (TA) in the fields of education and youth training. In particular it evaluates the role of the MSC/TA in the promotion and instutionalization of 'vocationalism' and 'enterprise culture'. Much recent literature has focused attention on the growth of 'new vocationalism' as a response to high levels of youth unemployment (Bates *et al.*, 1984; Brown and Ashton, 1987; Coles, 1988a; Pollard *et al.*, 1988; Raffe, 1988a). Less attention has been given to the activities of the MSC/TA in promoting 'enterprise' (Rees, 1986). The chapter will argue that the rationale, organization and mode of delivery for 'enterprise initiatives' illustrates a new and changing role for the TA in managing social and economic change.

In describing the development of cultures such as 'enterprise' or 'new vocationalism' five interrelated elements must be involved (Coles, 1988a). Firstly, we have a detailed understanding of the institutional innovations themselves. We will argue that apparently separate programmes in different institutional areas reflect a more general pattern. Not all the individual programmes which constitute 'vocationalism' and 'enterprise' can be covered in detail in this chapter. Rather, we have taken specific examples from youth training and education to illustrate how particular schemes reflect the more general trends of 'vocationalism' and 'enterprise'.

Secondly, we must pay close attention to the changing structural relationships which the initiatives have brought about: relationships of advice, consultation and policy making, the monitoring of aims and objectives, and methods of attaining financial control. Here we trace the ways in which the

MSC/TA have developed management strategies which have increasingly shifted power and control towards private industry.

Thirdly, we must directly examine 'cultures' — the rationale underpinning schemes and initiatives, the values they espouse and try to promote, together with the procedures through which schemes and initiatives are developed, delivered and legitimized. This 'culture' gives shape and direction to what, in administrative terms, may be discrete, sometimes almost *ad hoc*, policy initiatives.

Fourthly, we must examine the economic context in which changes occur. It is clear, for instance, that the development of 'new vocationalism' was stimulated by steep rises in youth unemployment in the 1970s. In the current promotion of 'enterprise', however, it should be recognized at the outset that *nationally* there is now a very different economic context. Repeated government White Papers on employment now see the major problem facing the country as being 'skill shortage' rather than unemployment (White Papers, 1988a and 1988b). We will argue that 'new vocationalism' and the promotion of 'enterprise culture' must be understood as responses to these different economic contexts.

Fifthly, close attention must be given to the ways in which nationwide initiatives articulate with local conditions. National 'blueprints' rarely simply reproduce themselves at a local level. Rather, they become mediated through local cultures and economic contexts (MacDonald, 1988a). In the final section of this chapter we will focus attention on Cleveland which, whilst having high rates of unemployment, has also become a key test site for 'enterprise' initiatives. First, we turn to the promotion of 'vocationalism' in youth training and education.

Youth Unemployment and the Growth of Youth Training

The growth of Youth Training provision has been well documented elsewhere (Atkinson and Rees, 1982; Brown and Ashton, 1988; Raffe, 1988a; Ainley, 1988). The Youth Training Scheme (YTS) has been referred to as 'the jewel in the MSC crown' (Finn, 1986a). It is, however, the culmination of a series of youth unemployment measures reaching back almost to the foundations of the MSC in 1974. In these early days the MSC saw its role as helping the young unemployed to compete more successfully with adults for work in an increasingly competitive labour market. What made them uncompetitive was the lack of experience of work and this, of course, at the time, required employment. 'Special measures' through work experience programmes (WEP) attempted to break the cycle. Despite these measures, however, youth unemployment in the mid 1970s continued to grow; and so, too, did the number and variety of schemes.

The Holland Report set the scene for the development of youth training throughout the 1970s and 1980s and provided the basic framework for the main precursor of YTS, the Youth Opportunities Programme (YOP) (Department of Employment, 1977). There are several elements to note in the diagnosis of 'the problem' made by Holland and the consequent approach to policy formation. Firstly, the issue of youth unemployment was seen as both a 'demand side' and a 'supply side' problem. There was a worry about the demand for youth labour in part because of competition from adults. The answer to this was to give young people skills and work experience. Secondly, there was a problem concerning the 'lumpiness' of supply; it was not spread evenly throughout the year. 'Training' could, therefore, be used as a form of seasonal 'warehousing' of young people until such time, during the year, that demand picked up. Thirdly, there was an acceptance of 'supply side deficiency' — the young unemployed were unqualified, and considered to be unprepared for the world of work, poorly motivated and displaying the wrong attitudes. The young unemployed were, thus, regarded as being the problem and as such *they* needed to be 'remedied'.

Fourthly, Holland recognized the need for a large scale nationwide network through which training could be delivered. Even a large bureaucracy like the MSC could not do this alone. The Report argued for a 'single, coherent programme, comprehensive in its coverage and responsive to the differing needs of unemployed young people in different parts of the country' (3.1b). To deliver such a programme the MSC considered it expedient, at least in the short term, to give training agents, in both the public and private sectors, power and initiative in the hope that this would provoke responsibility and involvement. They were to be left in charge of the management of funding.

The content of YOP was not outlined in the Holland Report. What emerged was a variable mixture of three core ingredients: work experience, skills training and social and life skills teaching. These were to remain the staple diet of youth training for the next ten years.

On most criteria YOP was failing by the early 1980s. It all but destroyed the youth labour market for 16-year-olds in a few short years whilst presiding over rapidly increasing rates of youth unemployment. The number of 16-year-olds with jobs fell from 61 per cent in 1974 to 18 per cent in 1984 (Roberts *et al.*, 1988). By 1982 the number of 16-year-olds on schemes accounted for more than a fifth of the age group (Raffe and Courtenay, 1988). But of those who entered schemes between June 1980 and July 1981, only 31 per cent entered employment as they completed them (Bedeman and Courtenay, 1982). YOP did, though, have an impact on the young unemployed themselves. The evidence suggests that, in the early years, YOP was successful in first 'blaming' and then 'remedying' the victims (Stafford, 1981; Atkinson and Rees, 1982). In this the 'social and life skills' elements, which found a place in all YOP programmes, played a critical part. Much of this was done through further education colleges. Staff were, of course, in no position to do anything about the lack of jobs for the young unemployed. They were, therefore, inevitably bound to concentrate on trying to groom the *particular* young people under their charge, despite the knowledge that this would do little to change the fortunes of young people *in general*. Ann Stafford comments:

> Given the structural limitations of the teaching situation, teachers can only act in an individualistic and pragmatic way . . . Faced with twelve jobless young people, the immediate task is to increase their [young people's] employability. This leads inevitably to a reinforcement and perpetuation of an individualistic explanation for unemployment . . . in unexpected ways and often in ways quite foreign to their well meaning intentions (Stafford, 1981, p. 62).

Despite its unpopularity with many young people YOP survived through the volatile years of the late 1970s and early 1980s, a period which also saw the election of the first Thatcher Government. By that time the *pattern* of training provision had been set.

By 1982 many YOP trainees had begun to vote with their feet, believing their contemporaries (rather than the commercials), that YOP was 'slave labour' and exploitation leading to the dole, rather than being a training bridge between school and a permanent job (Hughes, 1984; Coles, 1986). But YOP could not be abandoned without finding something to fill the gap. An MSC consultative paper, *A New Training Initiative*, in May 1981 urged:

As a country, we must now set ourselves the aim of achieving urgent and radical changes in our training arrangements if our industry and commerce and our workforce — both young and old — are to be adequately equipped to face the future (para.23).

A Youth Task Group was set up with the responsibility to report by April 1982. This described a scheme aimed at 460,000 16–17-year-olds (about 25 per cent of the age cohort). They were to be guaranteed a place on a twelve-month training scheme and offered 'an integrated programme of training, work experience and relevant education' (para.4.10). This was to be piloted in 1982–3 and come on 'full stream' in Autumn 1983. It did — just — make its deadlines, with many key personnel receiving guidelines, manuals and recruits in reverse order. In 1983 a quarter of the age group reaching the age of 16 was recruited to YTS. Training, under YTS, was described as 'high quality', but the nine components largely provided the old mix: work experience, training in particular work skills and 'personal effectiveness training'. Still youth unemployment continued to grow and by 1985, when YTS2 had been introduced, 25 per cent of the age group were being offered a two year period of training (Jones *et al.*, 1988). By then a large and competitive youth training industry had been established, but in 1985, the rules of the game had begun to change.

The Changing Shape of the Youth Training Industry

In the seven years between 1978 and 1985 'youth training' expanded by more than five-fold. Simultaneously with the growth in numbers there was an increase in the duration of training, from twelve-week courses in the mid-1970s, to a twenty-four-month programme under YTS2. The youth training industry is now so large and complex that a multitude of individuals and organizations are dependent upon it for their livelihood. New staff and new layers of organization have sprung up to cope with youth training. Many large companies have youth training sections to act as managing agents for their trainees. The old training boards (soon to be abolished or privatized) now have youth training sectors managing YTS. Elsewhere special companies such as 'Link' and 'Sight and Sound' have sprung up to provide the organization and delivery of youth training to clusters of smaller firms. This continues to be big business. Money can be made (and lost) by the efficient (parsimonious) management of MSC/TA income for YTS. Colleges of further education have become committed, in buildings, staff and resources to YTS provision. The temporary, last minute, employment of part-time staff, which was the pattern of the 1970s, changed to much more established and permanent staffing by the mid-1980s (Broomhead and Coles, 1988). In all these sectors personnel are dependent upon MSC/TA monies to pay their wages and the continued existence of the schemes to justify their jobs.

In introducing two year YTS, starting in 1985, the MSC attempted to build upon the fact that all the above organizations were beholden to them. It began to tighten its control. Training was restricted to those agencies which attained the status of 'Approved Training Organization' fulfilling requirements laid down by the MSC (Baddely, 1985). The 'Mode B' schemes disappeared and with them the block grant which had previously given significant extra financial support to specially protected schemes, particularly in the public sector. An 'incumbency payment system' was introduced which served to make financial planning difficult. Both these changes had an adverse impact on schemes and training providers in the public sector (Broomhead and Coles, 1988).

What also has to be recognized is that the expansion of youth training was expedient and 'from the bottom up' and initially devised for the largely unqualified 'bottom' 10 per cent of the age cohort (Atkinson and Rees, 1982). But YTS2 is being delivered to a client group of very mixed abilities. The unqualified remain one segment, but trainees also include within their ranks school-leavers with five or more O levels or their equivalent (Jones *et al.*, 1988).

But did this apparent massive expansion change the nature of youth training? The training component of YTS is flexible and many private sector employers, especially large employers, merely took the subsidy and carried on recruiting and training in the way in which they would have done had government schemes never been invented (Roberts *et al.*, 1986). In 1989, now that trainees are in short supply, the Training Agency has indicated that there can be much more flexibility in applying the rules about off-the-job training (*Times Educational Supplement*, 3 February 1989). But if large companies and the training boards have been allowed to pick up the subsidies, demand their own terms and largely ignore the diktats from the MSC/TA, this is certainly not true of local authorities, colleges of further education and the charities. This is the very partnership which has been involved in youth unemployment measures from the beginning, but from being welcome partners in 1978 they became, after 1985, a destabilized fringe (Broomhead and Coles, 1988).

As demographic changes begin to bite further into the size of the 16-year-old cohort in the 1990s, what then? The public sector vanguard of the training industry, conjured up in the 1970s to deal with youth unemployment, may be left without a client group. If, as Roberts has argued, the private sector has responded to youth training by 'taking the money and running', largely as it always has done, the public sector, under pressure from the change of rules in 1985, has had to run much faster, to stand still (Roberts *et al.*, 1986). As youth unemployment began to wane after 1985, its client group was beginning to be recruited by private sector schemes as all sections of the training industry trawled down-market. In the training field it is, therefore, very difficult to reach a single, simple assessment which describes the role played by the MSC. It has changed its tactics from year to year, mainly in response to unemployment levels. But it is clear that Government is increasingly convinced that *private industry* can supply the *most* appropriate training.

Vocationalizing Education

On 18 October 1976, Prime Minister James Callaghan made his now famous address to Ruskin College. In it he made it clear that education was no longer to be regarded as an end in itself. It was to be evaluated according to how well it prepared young people for the world of work. The (so-called) Great Debate which followed this speech brought few immediate consequences. The Thatcher Government has, however, used both 'carrot' and 'stick' politics to make education bend to the perceived needs of industry. Two contrasting cases of educational reform will be reviewed here as an illustration of how the MSC was employed to deliver 'vocationalism' in education.

The TVEI Story

The story of the Technical and Vocational Educational Initiative (TVEI) is perhaps the most dramatic of the stories which outline the birth and rapid expansion of 'new vocationalism' (Dale, 1985a; Gleeson, 1987). It arrived with little prior warning in 1982, the year after the launch of *A New Training*

Initiative (NTI). The consultative paper on NTI had obliquely signalled that the education service was in the sights of ministers (or civil servants) concerned about skill training. On 12 November 1982 Mrs Thatcher announced to the House of Commons that her Government intended to launch a new initiative for 14–18-year-olds designed to promote better technical and vocational education. The MSC was to establish a small number of pilot projects. The launch of TVEI was a closely guarded secret. The first MSC staff heard of their imminent involvement with this educational initiative was when TVEI was announced over the Moorfoot Tannoy on 12 November.

David Young, then chairman of the MSC, wrote to Local Education Authorities (LEAs) outlining the aims and objectives of the scheme in January 1983:

> First, our general objective is to widen and enrich the curriculum in a way that will help young people to prepare for the world of work and develop skills and interests including creative abilities that will help them to lead a fuller life and be able to contribute more to the life of the community. Secondly, we are in the business of helping students to learn. In a time of rapid technological change the extent to which particular occupational skills will be required will change. What is important about the initiative is that youngsters should receive an education which will enable them to adapt to the changing occupational environment (David Young quoted in Wilson, 1988, p. 148).

This was all pretty vague stuff; there was certainly nothing in the general statements to which most educationists would object. All applications for TVEI contracts were also required to fulfil nine criteria. Some of these were general educational objectives requiring 'a four year curriculum (fourteen-to-eighteen) designed as a preparation for adult life in a society liable to rapid changes' and 'preparation for nationally recognised qualifications'. Others were more specifically vocational, requiring the programme to include 'vocational and technical, as well as general educational elements', 'relevance to potential employment opportunities', 'work experience' and 'links with further training and education'. Many schools saw little that was objectionable in these; indeed, they positively welcomed other criteria which committed them to 'the provision of equal opportunities for both sexes and for ethnic minorities' and 'an emphasis upon personal development particularly in terms of initiative and the ability to solve problems'. Contrary to much popular opinion, many educationalists are not against the use of school time for 'work experience' and many are delighted at the opportunity to make school work 'relevant' and 'problem solving' and to use computers rather than 'chalk and talk' methods in their teaching. Indeed, many headteachers were delighted to have the opportunities *and resources* to shake some of their more complacent colleagues into being more adventurous in their approach to education and learning (Wilson, 1988). The only real suspicion was that the initiative was being funded by the MSC and not the Department of Education and Science (DES), and, not for the last time, educational purists were seen to wring their hands and mutter 'If you sup with the devil take care to do so with a long spoon'.

Bids for TVEI had to be received by the end of the first week in March 1983. Successful applicants were required to start the scheme in September of the same year. The £250m budget allocated for TVEI was certainly attractive, and those local authorities who agreed to 'pilot' the scheme were given the lion's share of the resources. In the first year £46m was promised to the first fourteen schemes approved. Rapid calculations indicated that specific schools could expect a massive injection of funds. Bradford, for instance, received £3.5m for its two school scheme (Wilson, 1988). When these sorts of incentives are dangled in front of LEAs and headteachers it is not surprising that they think carefully about how their long cherished ambitions can be eligible for MSC support. Sixty-six local authorities responded by the deadline.

TVEI was initially planned as an experiment and careful research monitoring was part of the package. But given the demand, it was easy to see why it could be expanded quickly before any genuine evaluation of its effectiveness could be made. By 1985 TVEI was running in every LEA in the country and by 1987 every school was eligible to apply to join. Funding for later schemes is far less lavish than for the initial ones. Less than half as much is being provided for the extension to *all* schools than was provided for the first fourteen schemes. Those who joined the initiative late in the day, however, are expected to learn from the experiences of the early pioneers.

This tactic of generous early funding has become one of the hallmarks of MSC/TA involvement in education. It entices education in a particular direction, but once set on that path education is left to resource itself. A similar tactic of 'wedge funding' is used to fund Professional Industrial and Commercial Updating (PICKUP) initiatives.

As might be envisaged, given the 1983 brief for TVEI, the actual patterns of development varied considerably between schemes (Gleeson, 1987). Some schools have embraced TVEI and used it as an opportunity completely to change their approach to teaching and learning throughout the school. Others have merely used TVEI as a minor 'bolt-on' extra to a school system which has remained, otherwise, predominantly unchanged. TVEI programmes are, however, *intended* to spread their influence, and detailed plans for doing this are now a requirement of TVEI contracts.

The next two years will be critical in assessing the impact of TVEI, and there are contradictory signs. There was not a single mention of TVEI in the 1988 Education Reform Act. Many saw this as indicating that Kenneth Baker was more concerned with standards for the elite in schools rather than the involvement of the masses (Coles, 1988b). But the systems of assessment and 'profiling' pioneered under TVEI do look likely to be introduced to all schools through the assessment systems proposed for the National Curriculum (Black, 1988). A number of the national curriculum subject reviews also indicate that some of the cross disciplinary project work developed through TVEI-based educational innovation may soon become the norm in all our schools (Black, 1988).

The Non-Advanced Further Education (NAFE) Story

Of all the White Papers on Education and Training of the 1980s it was *Training for Jobs*, published in January 1984, which proclaimed 'vocationalism' in the bluntest of terms. It started with simple dictums:

> 1. Britain lives by the skill of its people. A well trained work force is an essential condition of our economic survival.
> 2. But training is not an end in itself . . . Training must therefore be firmly work-oriented and lead to jobs.

By paragraph 8 it had reached the point where it was prepared to make assertions which caused consternation, even in the mildest of Conservative controlled local education authorities.

> 8. Training is an investment. It must be seen to pay for itself . . . Thus decisions as to who is trained, when and in what skills are best taken by employers.

We have already seen that this practice was already largely taking place in YTS and was to be further encouraged with the rule changes for YTS2 in 1985. But *Training for Jobs* did not just deal with YTS. It turned its attention to 'vocational education' undertaken in colleges of further education:

43. If the important developments described in this White Paper are to be carried through successfully, public sector provision for training and vocational education must become more responsive to employment needs at national and local level. The public sector needs a greater incentive to relate the courses it provides more closely to the needs of the customer and in the most cost effective way . . .

It should perhaps be noted that the 'customer' being referred to here was not the student, but the potential employer of trained labour. The paper continued:

45. For this purpose we have decided to give the Commission important new responsibilities by enabling it to purchase a more significant proportion of work-related non-advanced further education provided by local education authorities.
46. . . . The intention is therefore that the Commission should by 1986–87 account for about one quarter of the total provision in this area.

This led to a bitter quarrel between central and local government. Tory Shires were (not for the last time) outraged at this interference in educational provision. The MSC had not sought to adjudicate in such a bitter fight between central and local government, but they were given no room for compromise. Starting in 1986 local education authorities had to apply to the MSC for funds to run the Further Education system (25 per cent of the total budget), where previously such finance came to them automatically through the Rate Support Grant. In applying for funding, they have to do so in terms laid down by the MSC/TA. This means that the TA now defines the terms through which educational accounting should take place, and the legitimacy of the criteria used in educational planning. It is no good teachers and lecturers simply dreaming up interesting new courses, no matter how popular or fascinating their content may be. Such courses can only be mounted if a college can demonstrate that it will meet the needs of local industry. That is what the MSC rules say (MSC/LAA Policy Group, 1986). Because of the asymmetrical power relationship between educationalists and the MSC/TA, the whole culture of educational thinking has been forced to change (Broomhead and Coles, 1988).

The Advent of Enterprise

Whereas Callaghan's Ruskin Speech in 1976 and the Holland Report of 1977 can be regarded as critical milestones in the development and institutionalization of 'new vocationalism', the promotion of a 'culture of enterprise' has much less clear cut origins. Yet the promotion of such a culture is now busily under way across almost the full range of training and educational institutions. 'Enterprise projects' have now reached schools, colleges, YTS, ET, and higher education. By no means all of these are funded and managed by the Training Agency. Where projects were already under way ('Young Enterprise' in schools or 'Livewire' funded by Shell, for instance), the TA seems content to leave such projects well alone. But in areas where it has clear responsibility, particularly on training schemes, the promotion of 'enterprise culture' has become one of the key axes of change in the late 1980s. Rather than present a full review of the range of initiatives here we will first briefly outline the development of enterprise in just two contrasting institutional areas, the Youth Training Scheme and institutions of higher education.

Enterprise in YTS

One of the major changes in YTS in the late 1980s is the attempt to graft 'enterprise training' on to the scheme. In announcing the initiative, the minister, John Lee, argued that this was not simply an extra component to be added to the YTS aims and objectives. He heralded it as 'one of the most exciting initiatives undertaken by the MSC', one which was to be given 'high priority' and which would 'mark an important change in the thrust of training for young and old alike across all parts of our industrial and commercial life'. The outline of 'enterprise culture' and its significance was achieved by reference to its opposite 'the culture of dependency'.

In an Enterprise culture people create opportunities rather than wait for someone else to act. They have skills to generate wealth and resources rather than be dependent upon others. They have confidence to use their initiative rather than being powerless to take initiatives. People take advantage of change rather than remain confused by new situations and events . . . We want young people to gain the habits of looking for opportunities and not obstacles while they are in YTS. Habits which will stand them in good stead throughout their working lives (Regional MSC Conferences on 'Enterprise in YTS': published script).

These sentiments have become distilled into the six key elements of 'enterprise training' in YTS:

(i)   displaying initiative
(ii)   making decisions
(iii) managing resources
(iv)   displaying drive and determination
(v)   influencing others
(vi)   monitoring progress.

But 'enterprise' in YTS is not merely a new agenda for training. It is intended to be a new modality through which training is delivered. The trainer is to become a 'facilitator' rather than teacher; learning is to be 'active' rather than passive; and the process is to be closely integrated into systems of 'assessment' and 'profiling'. Trainees under 'enterprise training' are encouraged to develop 'self diagnoses', 'action plans' and 'self-appraisal' of what they gain from their training. The whole package is to be geared to nationally agreed systems of assessment and the 'action plans' and certificates of 'modules of competence' filed away as a permanent record in a NROVA (National Record of Vocational Achievement) file. NROVA certification is set to become the norm across all institutions of training and education, so that soon even university applicants will expect admission tutors to scrutinize the contents of their NROVA portfolio rather than merely count A level grades.

Enterprise in Higher Education (EHE)

After the 1987 General Election, it became clear that the Government was intent upon transforming higher education. The Enterprise in Higher Education (EHE) Initiative was launched in December 1987 by the Secretary of State for Employment with the support of the Secretaries of State for Education and Science, Trade and Industry, Scotland and Wales. The initiative is to be managed by the Training Agency. Institutions of HE are being offered up to £1m over five years to bring 'enterprise' into the undergraduate curricula. Over 100 institutions submitted bids for EHE money and in 1988 the first eleven institutions had projects under way. 'Supping with the devil' is thus becoming fashionable even in institutions of HE.

The rhetoric through which EHE is being promoted has a familiar ring. Adaptability to a rapidly changing world is to be encouraged amongst all students. They are to be taught 'how to learn' and 'how to apply a body of knowledge' rather than merely absorb an established body of facts and theories. Learning is to become a more active process, with more use of educational technology and practical project work. As with TVEI, many educationalists welcome these required elements of EHE as virtues they would wish to pursue anyway. But EHE promotes these, not as educational values in their own right, but as necessary to the development of skills demanded by industry. The 1989 review of the initiative states clearly that its aim is to use higher education as a vehicle for social engineering *in the interests of employers*:

> The workplace of today and tomorrow requires employees who are resourceful and flexible and who can adapt quickly to changes in the nature of their skills and knowledge. They will need to be able to innovate, recognise and create opportunities, work as a team, take risks and respond to challenges, communicate effectively and be computer literate. These attributes are the core skills of an enterprising person and lie at the heart of enterprising culture . . . The cornerstone of the initiative apart from enterprise itself is partnership. EHE makes possible a substantial and productive role for employers and practitioners so that they can become involved in the work of institutions, particularly in curriculum design, delivery and assessment (Training Agency, 1989, pp. 3, 4).

Many of the educational aims of EHE seem laudable. What remains of concern is the role to be played by industrialists in this new partnership being funded by TA.

Enterprise in Cleveland: 'Unemployment Remains the Major Issue'

So far we have traced the growth of 'vocationalism' and the advent of 'enterprise' at a national level. Our framework for analysis, however, stresses that national blueprints are often significantly modified as they are implemented at a local level. We now turn to a brief description of the philosophy and practices of 'enterprise' in an area of high unemployment, Cleveland. At a national level we will argue that, whilst 'vocationalism' initiatives were propelled along by high rates of unemployment, 'enterprise' initiatives are designed to take hold in an era, and in a context, in which unemployment is not the most pressing concern. Cleveland, then, represents a context in which there is a particularly heightened tension between the two philosophies of 'vocationalism' and 'enterprise'.

In two successive White Papers on Employment in 1988 the Government triumphantly pointed to significant reductions in unemployment and, politically, unemployment is fast disappearing as the major issue of highest national priority (White papers, 1988a and 1988b). Cleveland County Council, however, in *its* 1988 review of the state of the local economy, concluded '. . . unemployment remains the major issue in Cleveland' (Cleveland County Council Research and Development Unit, 1988). Cleveland, perhaps more than any other area, has experienced the most dramatic consequences of economic recession and industrial restructuring. A once thriving local economy, traditionally dependent on steel and chemical production, has more recently become famous for having the highest levels of unemployment in mainland Britain:

> This area has experienced a spectacular and remarkable collapse. The last two decades have seen Teesside transformed from an area with the greatest hopes for expansion and dynamism through massive investment in a thriving and relatively modern industrial base, to one with the highest rates of unemployment (at County level) in Great Britain (Foord *et al.*, 1985, pp. 2–3).

The situation of school-leavers and young people in Middlesbrough and Cleveland is particularly grim. Despite recent falls, nationally and locally, in the total number of unemployed, the proportion of school-leavers entering full-time employment in Cleveland was the lowest ever recorded in 1988 (approximately 6 per cent). Over the past three years the proportion of Middlesbrough school-leavers whose 'first destination' after leaving school was unemployment has actually increased from 9.5 per cent to nearly 15 per cent in 1988, as recorded by the Careers Service. The respective figures for Cleveland as a whole are 4.5 per cent in 1985 and 8.4 per cent in 1988. The national picture of recovery from recession, the end of unemployment and a booming economy, seems slow to reach Cleveland. The major 'option' for 16-year-old leavers is YTS. Over 70 per cent of the 1987 school-leavers joined YTS, but unfortunately this did not prove to be the much vaunted 'bridge to full-time work'. YTS progression statistics indicate that, in Cleveland, the majority of YTS trainees complete their scheme only to move from scheme to unemployment. Only 17 per cent enter employment from YTS on recent estimations (Cleveland County Council Careers Service, October 1988).

The economic collapse of Teesside over the last twenty years has, therefore, severely disrupted the movement of young people from school to work. Nor do recent falls in the local *overall* unemployment rates seem to have widened opportunities for youth employment. Reductions in national unemployment rates disguise the continuing impact youth unemployment has for transitions in this local labour market. The most obvious solution to continued high levels of unemployment would be, as the County Council itself has pointed out, '. . . the provision of permanent full-time work at an adequate rate of pay' (Cleveland County Council, 1987, p. 6). But this is not in tune with current Government emphasis upon the encouragement of self-reliance and the discouragement of dependency upon the efforts of others. Cleveland has become a, if not *the*, centre afor the development and testing of the Thatcher Government's strategy of encouraging 'enterprise'.

In reviewing 'enterprise' in Cleveland we will not focus on EHE or 'enterprise in YTS' but on the development of a separate 'enterprise industry'. A plethora of organizations has sprung up, phoenix-like, from the ashes of Cleveland's economic decline, to deliver the new gospel of enterprise to the young adults of the County. At the last count there were over eighty agencies and organizations concerned with youth enterprise in Cleveland. These provide enterprise training for school pupils (pre- and post-16), for trainees on

YTS, for the unemployed in Employment Training and for the self-employed on the Enterprise Allowance Scheme.

The organizations delivering or 'facilitating' enterprise training can be seen as composing a continuum. At one extreme there are important agencies offering advice, counselling and guidance toward cooperative and community based enterprise projects. Typical of such provision is the CREATE organization which operates according to a *broad* definition of 'enterprise'. Here enterprise is understood as: '. . . making things happen. It refers to the willingness and ability of people to be self determining and flexible, influencing, shaping and taking control over their own lives in any sphere, be that social, personal, economic or political' (CREATE publicity material).

If this is the 'left' end of the enterprise continuum, then the majority of structures, agencies and schemes lie to the 'right'. These may vary in terms of size, and the particular 'client group' they deal with, but they are united by two common factors. Firstly, they receive financial backing, at least in part, from the public purse, via the Training Agency. Secondly, they promote a much *narrower* version of enterprise. This equates 'enterprise' with self-employment. Through a variety of administrative bodies and schemes, but through the Enterprise Allowance Scheme (EAS) in particular, young people are encouraged to leave the 'dependency' of unemployment and to become 'their own boss'. This self-employment model of 'enterprise' is delivered in training courses lasting anything from one day to eight weeks; the topics for the training agenda being the basics of capitalist business development: marketing strategies, profit margins, and cash-flows, etc. There is little room within this conception of 'enterprise culture' for less competitive, less individualistic, but more cooperative or collective views of enterprise as a solution to unemployment.

Cleveland Youth Business Centre (CYBC), as its name suggests, is a typical example of this approach to enterprise. Its multimillion pound budget has been supported by the Training Agency, an 'Inner City Task Force' (the North Central Middlesbrough Task Force), local government and the private sector. It aims to provide: 'a valuable, one stop shop, for all young entrepreneurs providing essential, continuous support and advice to develop a viable business from the seed of an idea' (CYBC publicity material). Effectively what this means is a three stage process offering 'counselling', 'training', 'starter unit space' and 'backup services' for those prepared to enter self-employment. At the first stage, the intending young entrepreneurs are advised about their business ideas. Secondly, they are offered specific training courses in business skills. Thirdly, CYBC offers offices and workspace, at subsidized rates, through which enterprises can operate. This is further supplemented by on-going support including advice on marketing, book-keeping, the availability of grants and loans, etc.

CYBC is, of course, heavily reliant for clients upon the Enterprise Allowance Scheme. The EAS first became available in August 1983. It is this initiative, in particular, which is designed to promote and deliver the 'enterprise culture' to young adults in Cleveland. To be eligible for the scheme applicants must have been unemployed and receiving benefit for eight weeks, have at least £1,000 to invest in a business, and be between the ages of 18 and 65. Further restrictions are that the applicant must be prepared to work full-time on the venture, it must be a new enterprise, and it must be 'suitable for public support' (i.e. not involving 'night clubs, licensed drinking clubs, . . . gambling, business which promotes political or religious views, or involve nude modelling, sex or pornography') (DE EAS Leaflet). As long as applicants can match these criteria, the EAS provides an allowance of £40 for 12 months, and provides free business advice and training (often through organizations such as CYBC). Though access is governed by these rules, the scheme is not controlled by any test that the proposed business is commercially viable. It is estimated that less than 4 per cent of applications for the scheme are rejected (Finn, 1986b). Given this, it is perhaps not surprising that nearly half of the 300,000 small businesses set up nationally under the EAS failed within three years, and about half also displaced existing businesses (National Audit Office Report, reported in *Guardian*, 9 March 1989). Disaggregated figures which would indicate the degree of success (or otherwise) in Cleveland are proving difficult to obtain, but it is unlikely that new businesses in this area, and businesses set up by young adults, are going to fare more successfully than the national figures indicate. Foord *et al.* make the following point:

> Setting up a new small business is hazardous and often leads to failure, especially in areas like Teesside. The 'enterprise culture' of self employment which Ministers talk of can hardly be expected to develop in an area which big business and nationalised industries are abandoning (Foord *et al.*, 1986, p. 45).

A particular problem in assessing the impact of 'enterprise' and self-employment in Cleveland is 'multiple auditing'. Many of the organizations promoting 'enterprise' have to operate within a culture of TA monitoring. This demands quantification of 'success' and justifies continuation of funding on a 'payment by results' basis. Thus a particular, 'successful' individual entrepreneur is likely to be counted several times by different organizations as evidence of *their* success, even if contact with the client has been minimal. But the reliance on quantification of outcome has another important effect. If the narrow version of 'enterprise' is employed then, despite 'multiple auditing', there are clear and measurable outcomes — business 'start up' and business 'survival rates'. If, however, the wider philosophy and practice of enterprise is promoted then 'outcome' is a much more nebulous concept. Organizations like CREATE work with a much broader measure of 'success' as 'positive outcome'. This *may* eventually be self-employment, or a completed community project (such as organizing a social outing), but equally a 'positive outcome' of enterprise activities could mean increased feelings of self-efficacy and self worth among unemployed clients. Clearly this makes it much more difficult to measure 'success' and justify the existence of organizations employing the broader definition of 'enterprise' to funding bodies such as the TA.

The maze of organizations which has grown in Cleveland during the mid-1980s to deliver the 'enterprise culture' is directly and indirectly dependent upon Training Agency funding. Organizations have quickly been formed and immediately asked to deliver new schemes for changing client groups at short notice. The TA, like the MSC before it, is always in a hurry. Since September 1988, for instance, consortia with acronyms such as HANDS (Help and Development Support), FACE (Facility for Access to Creative Enterprise) as well as CYBC have been enticed to develop short, intensive 'enterprise training programmes' to mesh with Employment Training (ET) requirements. Some of these have been 'feeder' courses for 'enterprise rehearsal' (whereby a client can establish and run a business for a year under the auspices of an umbrella organization, like CYBC, which takes overall responsibility for such projects). Yet these are being managed without any clear concept of 'progression' beyond the end of the eight week course, and it is unclear what outcomes are possible if ET trainees then decide *not* to start their own businesses.

Furthermore, many of those employed to deliver these initiatives are themselves often in an insecure and vulnerable position. Many have gained their new found status as 'prophets of enterprise' only through previous involvement with the TA through the Community Programme. Others, particularly those in senior positions, are 'secondees' from local industry. But initial multi-million pound budgets are now being exhausted, and personnel are faced with having to seek out new means of keeping their organizations afloat. The funding of 'enterprise' initiatives, *and their own jobs*, is only short term. Rumours abound that many of the eighty-plus organizations will be 'rationalized' when the proposed new Training and Enterprise Councils (TECs), announced in the December 1988 Employment White Paper, are formed to oversee both youth and adult training. The other side of the coin, however, is that TECs will have an additional source of revenue. The 'Business Growth through Training' (BGT) initiative, also announced in the December 1988 White Paper, has been allocated a budget of £1.4 billion. This is an initiative for firms already in existence and is designed to produce a new 'invest in your workforce' and 'training throughout life' philosophy. But the White Paper *Employment in the 1990s* makes it clear that this BGT initiative will be directed at small businesses and owner-managers as well as at skill-shortages identified by TECs.

Conclusions

In the introduction we suggested that an assessment of the change from a culture of 'vocationalism' to a culture of 'enterprise' was best accomplished by employing a five point framework and it is to this that we now return.

Firstly, the literature on 'vocationalism', to which we referred earlier, suggests that it is a concern to make education and training accountable to the needs of industry which unites a range of schemes and initiatives, from YOP to YTS and TVEI together. Also of significance is that these are 'bottom up' innovations in which the budget and size of the initiative was largely determined by youth unemployment and that their major impact was in 'remedying' the unemployed (Stafford, 1981; Raffe, 1984c). 'Enterprise' projects, however, have a wider constituency. To be sure, many projects can still be seen as throwing money at the unemployment problem, as was demonstrated by the case of Cleveland. But 'enterprise culture' is now being directed at all sectors of education and training, the unemployed *and* the employed. In education, too, 'enterprise' is being cultivated in all schools and is designed to reach the very pinnacles of the universities' ivory towers. This shift from 'vocationalism for some' to 'enterprise for all' is, we suggest, an important change of direction.

Secondly, an examination of the pattern of institutional relationships being promoted by 'vocationalism' and 'enterprise' also indicates some marked similarities. The Training Agency is using the same strategies as the MSC before it to induce widespread and rapid change. 'Enterprise' is being piloted under a vague brief with 'wedge funding'. The results of pilots are intended to spread throughout institutions and plans for 'embedding' are now an important part of enterprise contracts. The TA is still a major means through which schemes are promoted and funded. But following the abolition of the Training Commission there are signs that the Training Agency itself may not be master of its own house for much longer. Rather, in the administration of training, TECs, made up of local representatives of business and commerce, are going to be in charge, with TA staff servicing TECs on secondment. Early signs indicate that the large budgets given to TECs (approximately £47 million, for instance, in Cleveland), have ensured that major employers *are* willing to take on and take over the control of training. Indeed, they have already indicated that they want to exercise even more power and control than was envisaged by the White Paper (*Times Educational Supplement*, 21 July 1989). The funding councils controlling higher education are similarly dominated by captains of industry. Together these developments give much more *direct* influence to industry to call the tune in future reforms of education and training.

Thirdly, the rhetorics of 'vocationalism' and 'enterprise' also display important differences. 'Vocationalism' was concerned with changing attitudes to work and industry. 'Enterprise' is concerned to facilitate and promote initiative, a flexible and constructive approach to problem solving, adaptability in using resources and self-monitoring and self-reliance. This may, of course, be no more than a change in linguistic packaging. More significant is the fact that institutional and personal economic survival is sometimes dependent on being prepared to frame tenders and contracts in 'TA-speak'. In many cases, as with YTS, this may be little more than playing language games in order to fund what the institution would wish to commit itself to anyway — a practice which Americans call 'boondoggle'. But because TA contracts are legal commitments, some still regard them as hostages to fortune.

Fourthly, we have argued here and elsewhere that the key to understanding the direction and speed of change is to be found in the economic context in which it occurs (Coles, 1988a). This we see as the most fundamental difference between the promotion of 'vocationalism' and 'enterprise'. The Government is repeatedly heralding the end of unemployment and pronouncing that the real need is now to break down 'the barriers to employment', for example by remedying inadequacies in training provision (White Paper, 1988b). Existing and anticipated skill shortages, the White Paper argues, result from failures to recognize 'investment in people' (unemployed *and* in work) as sufficiently important.

This appears to recognize the fifth point in our analytical framework. The White Paper argues that decisions as to who needs to be trained must be devolved to industrialists *at a local level* — where people work and are trained (para.4.8). It is for this reason that TECs will become the most significant institutions in the 1990s in determining the direction of change.

There are many long standing critics of Government training policy who might be expected to welcome, at least in part, these sentiments. Sociological studies of labour markets have, over the past decade, stressed the importance of *local* labour market conditions in determining the fortunes of young people (Ryrie, 1983; Ashton and Maguire, 1986; Roberts, Dench and Richardson, 1987; Coles, 1988a; MacDonald, 1988b). But there does appear to be a contradiction between this recognition of the importance of local factors and the continued promotion of major *national* initiatives. Employment Training claims to match the 'workers without jobs' to 'the jobs without workers', without recognition of the geography which divides the two halves of the equation. Similarly, as the discussion of the 'enterprise culture' in Cleveland suggested, 'enterprise' which *in general* may represent a shift in focus in training policy from the *unemployed* to the *employed*, is being heavily funded, in at least this area, as an unemployment measure.

It is this image of the Training Agency scurrying around promoting such apparent contradictions and anomalies in Government thinking which has led some critics to label it as an 'adhocracy' — 'an organization capable of sophisticated innovation deploy[ing] teams of experts in ad hoc projects' (Coffield, 1984, p. 29). But 'ad hocary' is sometimes seen as a virtue in enterprise culture, indicating a willingness to be flexible and adaptable in managing resources rather than being tied down by strict rules, regulations and procedures. But whilst this may be regarded as a virtue by Government, the Department of Employment and the Training Agency, the constant unpredictability of funding remains the basis for continuing uncertainty and insecurity in Cleveland's precarious 'enterprise industry'.

Note

1   Part of this chapter draws on work conducted under a project funded by the ESRC 16–19 Initiative on Youth and Enterprise in Cleveland. The research is being carried out by Robert MacDonald and Frank Coffield at the University of Durham. The views expressed here are, however, entirely those of the authors.

Acknowledgment

We would like to thank Mary Maynard for her helpful comments on drafts of this chapter.

Chapter 4

The Transition from YTS to Work: Content, Context and the External Labour Market

David Raffe

Introduction

The Transition from YTS to Work

The transition from school to work is not what it used to be. Over the last twenty years researchers in the area have had to come to terms with the rise in youth unemployment, with the discovery that half the people making the transition were female, with schemes for the unemployed, with the 'new vocationalism', with changes in qualifications, with the introduction of the Youth Training Scheme (YTS), with the abolition of youth unemployment through changes in benefit entitlement, and now with the prospect of shortages of young workers. These changes have stimulated increased research activity, although much of this has been descriptive and policy-driven and theoretical development has tended to lag behind. Nevertheless there has been increased interest from a variety of perspectives in understanding the longitudinal character of the transition process, and in exploring 'staged transitions', 'routes', and 'trajectories' (Jones, 1987; Wallace, 1987b; Roberts, 1987; Bynner, 1987; Clough *et al.*, 1988; Coles, 1988c; Roberts and Parsell, 1988a).

YTS plays a central role in this. A majority of young people entering the labour market at 16 pass through the scheme, which now provides a possible two-year stage between compulsory education and employment. The first stage of this new 'staged transition', that from school to YTS, has been studied in some detail. Researchers have examined the processes of selection and recruitment of young people onto YTS, the organization of schemes, the relation of prior educational, social, gender and ethnic divisions to differentiation within YTS, and trainees' attitudes to YTS. The second stage of this transition, from YTS to (un)employment, has been studied in less detail. Researchers have focused mainly on the proportions finding jobs; other dimensions of this transition, or the processes involved, have so far received less attention. This chapter attempts to fill this gap.

Internal and External Recruitment

The analysis in this chapter is based on two distinctions. The first is between internal and external recruitment from YTS. By 'internal recruitment' I mean recruitment by an employer organizing the trainee's scheme or providing work experience or another component of it. This is contrasted with 'external recruitment', by an employer not directly connected with the scheme.

Tacitly, much of the research and debate on YTS has assumed that internal recruitment is the key to the transition from YTS, and that most trainees who seek work in the external labour market are either 'rejects' who fail to be selected for internal vacancies or (disadvantaged) trainees from schemes which are too detached from the labour market to be used as sources of recruitment by employers. This assumption is reflected in the YTS-related research on employers (Hedges and Witherspoon, 1984; Chapman and Tooze, 1987; Roberts, Dench and Richardson, 1987; Sako and Dore, 1987; Deakin and Pratten, 1987). This research has examined the reasons for becoming involved in YTS, the costs and benefits of participation, and the relation to employers' own recruitment processes; the recruitment of young people from other employers' YTS schemes has been studied in much less detail, if at all. In the late 1970s and early 1980s school-leaver unemployment stimulated a massive research bid to investigate the influence of qualifications and other school outcomes on the selection of young workers (Manpower Services Commission, 1978; Hunt and Small, 1981; Ashton *et al.*, 1982; Livock, 1983). So far there has been no comparable study of the use of YTS outcomes as criteria for selecting young workers from the external labour market.

The distinction between internal and external recruitment loosely corresponds to Marsden and Ryan's (1988; Marsden, 1986, pp. 230–47) distinction between internal and occupational labour markets. (Unstructured or secondary markets are a third category.) Internal labour markets provide routes for career progression within the enterprise; much training is provided internally and occupational definitions, skill requirements and training standards may vary across enterprises. Occupational labour markets, by contrast, 'encourage the mobility of qualified workers amongst employers and work best with a system of standardised qualifications' (Marsden and Ryan, 1988, p. 1). YTS may be understood as part of a programme to establish competitive occupational labour markets in Britain (*ibid.*, pp. 13–14). The philosophy of YTS therefore emphasizes general and transferable skills. If these are not marketable in the general labour market then either YTS is failing to deliver these skills or the British youth labour market is failing to recognize or value them.

More immediately, YTS is fighting to maintain its position in a tightening youth labour market in the face of pressures on employers to reduce training and to use higher wages to attract 'good' young workers (NEDO, 1988; IDS, 1988). To this end it must not only persuade employers to continue to recruit through YTS, it must also persuade young people to prefer YTS placements to the higher wages and often greater security available in non-YTS jobs. This task of persuasion would be much easier if the skills gained through YTS were demonstrably marketable.

There are other, social and distributional, issues at stake. If the main avenue to employment offered by YTS is through being retained by a YTS employer, then selection at 16, to the 'right' scheme, remains critical. Selection on to the most sought-after YTS schemes, and the well-documented relation of ethnic, gender and social divisions to differentiation within YTS, will be lasting in their effects. Conversely, if eventual employment chances depend primarily on skills acquired on YTS, and especially if these skills are transferable across firms and even across occupations, then more of the burden of occupational selection can be delayed to 18 for the school-leavers who pass through YTS.

Content and Context

The second, and related, distinction made in this paper is that between the content and context of education and training. The distinction is discussed in detail elsewhere (Raffe, 1984d, 1987b). Applied to YTS, the notion of context 'refers to its articulation with structures of educational and occupational differentiation and, in particular, with selection and recruitment in the labour market' (Raffe, 1987b, p. 4). The *context* of YTS schemes may vary independently of their *content*, that is the quality and relevance of the knowledge, skills and competences gained therein. At least two aspects of their context are of interest here. First, YTS schemes give their trainees differential access to the information networks through which jobs may be found. Internal recruitment may be seen as a special case of recruitment through information networks. That is, young people who enter YTS schemes which are used as screening devices or recruitment pools by employers are thereby gaining access to informal recruitment networks. (This interpretation follows Jenkins *et al.*'s (1983) analysis of informal recruitment in terms of information flows.) However some YTS schemes provide access to external recruitment networks, by putting their trainees in touch with employers elsewhere (Knasel and Watts, 1987).

The second aspect of context which may vary independently of content relates to the signalling function of education and training (Spence, 1983). YTS schemes may acquire reputations for attracting 'good' trainees, or conversely they may be stigmatized as catering for the most disadvantaged or least employable young people. In addition, the fact that an unemployed young person has joined any YTS scheme may signal a positive attitude and motivation to a potential employer. Once again the signal is unrelated to the content of the scheme.

Figure 4.1: Modes of recruitment after YTS

Channel	Main source of YTS help
1. Internal	Context (contact with YTS employer: special case of information network)
2. External	Content (knowledge, skills and competences gained on YTS)
3. External	Context (access to external information network, or signal of pre-existing qualities)
4. External	No help from YTS

Figure 4.1 shows how the distinction between internal and external recruitment is related to the distinction between context and content. It shows four ways in which trainees may find full-time jobs after leaving a YTS scheme. First, they may be kept on in the internal labour market, with an employer associated with the scheme. Since the job would have arisen from the

contact with employers gained through YTS, it would have been gained primarily on the strength of the context of the scheme (or more precisely of the placement). Second, they may find a job externally on the strength of the scheme's content, that is of the knowledge, skills and competences acquired there. Third, they may find a job externally on the basis of the scheme's context, through introductions to other employers provided by scheme personnel, through the reputation of the scheme for attracting good recruits, or because participation on YTS signals motivation or desired personal qualities. Fourth, they may find a job largely independently of YTS. This chapter is particularly interested in the second of these modes. It asks to what extent young people find jobs in the external labour market on the strength of the content of YTS — seemingly a test of the quality and relevance of YTS training.

The notions of content and context are applied here at a micro-sociological level, in relation to individual employment chances. But their macro implications are equally if not more important. Current training policy puts its faith in the market (Department of Employment, 1988). Although reinforced by notions of 'flexibility' and 'industry leadership', this policy continues to be framed by a 'modified market model' of training (Raffe, 1987b, pp. 2–3). In this model the courses of training (or education) with the highest quality and most appropriate content are those that best help young people to get jobs, and to get good jobs. Market signals are thereby created that encourage young people (and especially the 'best' young people) to enter the best and most appropriate forms of training. However to the extent that employment chances depend on the context rather than the content of training (or education) the market signals will be distorted (*ibid.*, p. 4). Even with a subsidy to the supply of training, market forces will not suffice to ensure the best level or mix of training, as judged by economic, let alone educational criteria.

Recruitment to YTS

This chapter describes the experiences of a year group of young people who had been in fourth year of secondary school in Scotland (roughly equivalent to the English fifth year) in 1983/4. The data are from the Scottish Young People's Survey. A 10 per cent sample drawn from all secondary schools in

Scotland was sent postal questionnaires in spring 1985, spring 1986 and autumn 1987. The analysis below is based on the 50 per cent of the original target sample who responded to all three sweeps (n = 4013). Non-response bias is compensated by the use of design weights; the weighted sample is representative of the population in respect of gender, fourth-year qualifications and early leaving. Sample numbers reported in the tables are unweighted. It should be noted that the data are obtained from young people themselves, and cover only the one-year YTS. The implications of these limitations are discussed later.

More than 99 per cent of the year group had been eligible to leave school by the end of 1984. By the third survey sweep in autumn 1987 the average age of year-group members was more than 19 and most had completed compulsory education more than three years earlier; even those who had stayed on at school for an extra two years had been out of school for more than a year. A detailed account of the routes followed by sample members over this period is provided by Furlong and Raffe (1989).

All those who left school in 1984, and younger sample members who left in 1985, were unconditionally eligible for YTS, then still a one-year scheme. Those who left aged 17 in 1985 or 1986 were eligible but only if they were unemployed. Altogether 43 per cent of year-group members — 51 per cent of labour-market entrants — had at least started a YTS scheme by 1987. Those who entered the labour market before spring 1985 were much more likely to enter YTS (65 per cent) than later entrants (29 per cent). More males than females went on the scheme, but this was very largely explained by the tendency for males to enter the labour market earlier. Less qualified leavers were most likely to enter (67 per cent of labour-market entrants with no O or H passes, compared with 17 per cent of those with Highers passes) but this too was partly due to the tendency for less qualified leavers to enter the labour market earlier; among early entrants, participation on YTS was only weakly related to qualifications. Reinforcing many of these trends, the scale of YTS was greater in areas of higher unemployment.

Leaving YTS: Internal and External Labour Markets

On leaving their schemes, 34 per cent of YTS trainees found full-time jobs with scheme sponsors or work experience providers. I shall call these the 'internal recruits'. Four in ten (40 per cent) found jobs in the external labour market: I shall call them the 'external recruits'. They comprised 16 per cent who left their schemes early to take up their jobs, 8 per cent who entered jobs immediately on completing YTS, and 16 per cent who found external jobs after an initial spell of unemployment. One in six YTS trainees (17 per cent) became unemployed on leaving YTS and had still not found jobs by 1987. The remaining 9 per cent did not continue in the full-time labour market on leaving YTS, but entered part-time jobs (4 per cent), full-time education (2 per cent) or some other destination (3 per cent). A few of these had re-entered the full-time labour market and found jobs by autumn 1987, but they are excluded from subsequent analyses of 'internal' and 'external' recruits.

The external recruits found their jobs through a variety of channels, broadly similar to those used by young people who had found full-time jobs without going on YTS. The external recruits from YTS were less likely than the non-YTS recruits to have found out about jobs through advertisements in a newspaper (10 per cent compared with 15 per cent) or through contacting an employer directly (12 per cent compared with 26 per cent); 8 per cent of them had found out about their jobs through the managing agent or other people on their schemes, compared with none of the non-YTS recruits. But identical proportions (39 per cent) mentioned 'family or friends' as their source of information, and almost equal proportions (25 per cent and 24 per cent) mentioned Jobcentres or Careers Offices.

External Recruitment, Content and Context

The fact that the external recruits found their jobs through much the same channels as were used by non-YTS entrants to employment raises the question: how much difference did their YTS training make to the job-finding process? Table 4.1 shows the external recruits' responses to a question asking whether, and how, YTS had helped them to find jobs. The question did not refer specifically to their immediate post-YTS jobs; nearly a third had changed jobs since leaving YTS and this may account for the three 'external' recruits who responded that they had been taken on by their YTS sponsor or employer.

These data reflect the perceptions of young people and must be interpreted with caution. Young people would not necessarily have known whether their YTS experience influenced an employer's decision to hire them;

Table 4.1: 'In what ways, if any, has being on YTS helped you get a job?' by time of entry to job, and by whether in same or different occupation in 1987 (external recruits: percentages)

	All external recruits	Time of entry to job			If in full-time job in 1987	
		before completing YTS	on completing YTS	after initial unemployment	same occupation	different occupation
YTS has not helped me get a job	59	62	34	68	35	68
I was kept on by my YTS sponsor or employer	1	*	1	1	1	0
My YTS sponsor or supervisor told me about a job with a different employer	5	5	11	1	10	2
I heard about a job through other trainees on the scheme	2	2	3	1	1	3
The certificate or qualifications I got on YTS helped me get a job	10	6	18	9	14	8
I was offered a job because I'd done the same sort of job on YTS	16	16	28	12	28	13
The work experience I got on the scheme helped me get a job	22	23	41	13	43	16
The skills I learnt on the scheme helped me get a job	18	19	32	11	36	13
I was given a job because I'd been on YTS	5	4	5	6	7	3
It has helped in some other way	16	14	22	15	17	13
Any 'content'	32	30	58	21	54	25
n	(482)	(194)	(99)	(189)	(106)	(251)

Notes:
Respondents could tick as many items as applied. Those ticking none are excluded from the 100% base.
'Content': any of 'certificate or qualifications', 'same sort of job', 'work experience' or 'skills'.
'Same occupation': based on 24 Warwick Occupational Categories.

and some of the effects of YTS, for example in boosting self-confidence or changing attitudes to job search, may not have been perceived as help in getting jobs. Nevertheless it is a matter of concern that a majority (59 per cent) of YTS leavers who found employment in the external labour market (and by implication a larger majority of those who sought employment there) felt that their YTS training had not helped them to get a job. The young people most ready to acknowledge the help of YTS were those who had either entered employment on completing their schemes or continued in the same occupation.

We can identify three groups among the external recruits. The first comprises young people who said they had been helped by the *content* of their schemes, in the sense of the earlier discussion. Altogether 32 per cent of the external recruits referred to at least one of the following ways in which YTS had helped them: the certificate or qualifications, the (same) sort of job, the work experience or the skills they had learnt. A second and much smaller group mentioned none of these, but acknowledged one of the other kinds of help listed in Table 4.1. Some mentioned information networks to which they had gained access through YTS. Others said they had been 'given a job because I'd been on YTS'; since none of these mentioned any of the more obvious aspects of 'content' described above (had they done so they would have been allocated to the first group) it seems likely that the mere fact of their participation on YTS signalled a degree of motivation or a positive attitude to work or training. Others said they had been helped in 'some other way'. Altogether 15 per cent of the external recruits were in this second group, who mentioned at least one type of help that did not indicate the 'content' of YTS; we infer that they were helped by its 'context'. The third group comprises the 53 per cent of external recruits who ticked that 'YTS has not helped me get a job' and did not tick any of the other responses. (These are fewer than the 59 per cent shown in Table 4.1 because some of these, apparently contradictorily, ticked other items as well.)

To these three groups we must add a fourth group, of young people who ticked none of the responses in Table 4.1. (They are excluded from the 100 per cent base in the table.) Distinguishing these four groups among the external recruits enables us to produce a typology of 'leaving profiles' of YTS trainees. This is shown in Table 4.2. Only one in nine YTS leavers (11 per cent) found a full-time job in the external labour market on the strength of the 'content' of YTS. Many more found full-time jobs on the strength of its context, usually internally (10 per cent plus 24 per cent), but sometimes externally (5 per cent). And nearly one in five YTS leavers (19 per cent) found a job without the acknowledged help of YTS. All these proportions may be increased slightly if we allow for the 3 per cent of 'not knowns' and for those who did not continue in the full-time labour market after YTS but found jobs subsequently.

Table 4.2: YTS leaving profile, by gender (percentages)

	All	Males	Females
Internal recruitment:			
before completing scheme	10	7	14
on completing scheme	24	28	20
External recruitment helped by:			
content of YTS	11	9	14
context of YTS	5	5	6
not helped by YTS	19	23	15
not known	3	3	3
Unemployment, no full-time job by 1987	17	19	16
Others (incl. PT job, FT education)	9	7	13
Total	98	101	101
n	(1336)	(700)	(636)

I have described the internal recruits as finding jobs on the strength of their scheme's context. This is not to say that content was unimportant to them, rather that its relation to job selection was different. Typically, the content of the internal recruits' schemes was determined on the basis that they (or some of them) would get jobs, rather than job selection being determined on the basis of scheme content. Some trainees who found jobs with work experience providers (as distinct from managing agents responsible for the whole scheme) may have been helped by the skills acquired on YTS; but many of these left their schemes early, which suggests that the scheme content could not have been all that important, or was at least outweighed by the costs of continued YTS participation.

The specific question posed earlier in this paper was: to what extent do young people find jobs in the external labour market on the strength of the content of YTS? We can now answer it: about one trainee in nine finds a job in this way, or about one in three of external recruits. Such evidence as is available on the external marketability of YTS is consistent with these findings. For example only 19 out of a sample of 217 employers participating in YTS in 1986 noticed any general increase in the supply of skilled or experienced workers which could be attributed to YTS schemes other than their own (Deakin and Pratten, 1987, p. 495). In their entire sample of 308 YTS and non-YTS employers, Roberts *et al.* (1987a, p. 58) 'encountered just one employer who favoured applicants with YTS experience gained elsewhere'. More recently, a study of all new vacancies in Chesterfield in one week in July 1988 found that only 37 per cent of the employers concerned would consider a YTS-trained person sufficiently qualified for the job, despite the low skill level of most jobs on offer (Marsh, 1988, p. 23).

The external marketability of YTS may increase under the two-year scheme, although other current developments — notably the drive to encourage more 'employed status' participants on YTS — may encourage internal recruitment instead. The development most likely to encourage external recruitment on the basis of content is the extension of certification through YTS. All trainees will work towards qualifications approved by national 'lead industry bodies'. Four in ten YTS trainees in the present sample reported gaining qualifications (other than the YTS certificate) while on YTS. These trainees were slightly more likely than the others to be recruited externally with the help of content (14 per cent compared with 11 per cent) but they were also twice as likely to be recruited internally at the end of their schemes (34 per cent compared with 17 per cent). Interpretation of these comparisons is difficult, since certification was probably more often available on particular types of schemes with particular expected progression routes. Moreover, certification may be a necessary but not a sufficient condition for the external marketability of YTS training: other conditions must be fulfilled for occupational labour markets to be established and maintained (Marsden, 1986, pp. 239–47). One important condition is that employers must recognize vocational qualifications and use them as criteria in selection: a point to which I return later. The present data give no grounds for believing that the extension of certification alone will give more than a modest boost to the external marketability of the content of YTS.

Twice as many girls as boys were recruited internally before the end of their YTS scheme (Table 4.2). Among those recruited externally, girls were more likely to report that YTS had helped them find employment, and the largest difference was in the proportion mentioning some aspects of content. A substantial majority of boys finding work in the external labour market did not acknowledge any help from YTS.

Differentiated Patterns of Transitions from YTS

The first panel of Table 4.3 casts some light on these gender differences. It shows variation in leaving profiles across YTS schemes in broad occupational groups, aggregations of the 24 Warwick Occupational Categories (see Furlong and Raffe, 1989). The predominantly female clerical and secretarial schemes had the highest proportion of trainees recruited internally, nearly half of whom did not complete their schemes. The predominantly male craft and skilled manual group had the highest proportion finding jobs with scheme sponsors on completing their schemes; operatives and labourers, another disproportionately male group, had the next highest proportion. The overall proportion finding jobs externally varied relatively little across occupational areas, but the proportion doing so helped by the content of YTS varied much more. It was highest in respect of schemes in clerical and secretarial occupations (16 per cent) and personal service occupations (15 per cent). Significantly, these two categories include business studies and catering, which account for a large share of occupationally specific full-time college courses for this age group. Employers in most other occupational areas, it appears, are less used to recruiting 17- or 18-year-olds on the basis of occupational skills gained in pre-entry courses.

The category in Table 4.3 marked 'no codable occupation' includes some YTS schemes on which survey data were missing or incomplete, but it also includes schemes where the kind of training was too general or occupationally diverse to be coded into a single occupational category. Such schemes tended to be near the bottom of the informal status hierarchy of YTS schemes, and this is reflected in the low proportions of their trainees finding jobs either internally or in the external labour market with the aid of the content of YTS.

The variation in YTS leaving profiles across different school qualification groups partly reflected these occupational differences. Trainees with just one or two O grade passes were more likely to be recruited internally on completing their schemes, or recruited externally helped by the content of YTS, than the better qualified. The reason for this appeared to be the tendency for many better qualified trainees to be offered jobs by their scheme sponsors (or, more probably, work experience providers) before the end of their schemes. About half of all YTS trainees (51 per cent) were in the lowest qualification group, with no O grade or Highers passes. Half of these either became unemployed and had not found full-time employment by 1987 (27 per cent), or found jobs

Table 4.3: YTS leaving profile by occupation of YTS scheme, by SCE qualifications, and by date of entry to the full-time labour market (percentages)

	Internal recruitment		External recruitment helped by				Unemployment, no FT job by 1987	Others	Total	n
	before completing YTS	on completing YTS	content	context	not helped	NK				
Occupational group of YTS scheme										
Professional managerial & related	9	23	5	6	19	5	10	23	100	(49)
Clerical and secretarial	20	22	16	5	13	4	12	8	100	(344)
Sales	8	19	9	3	20	5	20	16	100	(186)
Personal service	8	20	15	6	19	2	15	15	100	(135)
Craft and skilled manual	4	33	9	5	25	3	17	4	100	(324)
Operatives and labourers	10	26	11	7	16	2	21	5	98	(231)
No codable occupation	9	4	4	8	27	4	29	15	100	(66)
SCE qualifications										
Highers	23	27	10	6	13	3	6	13	101	(133)
3+ O grades (A–C)	15	28	14	8	19	2	6	7	99	(337)
1–2 O grades (A–C)	9	31	16	6	15	5	10	8	100	(339)
No O or H	7	18	9	4	22	3	27	10	100	(524)
Date of entry to FT labour market										
By spring 1985	8	22	11	6	21	3	20	9	100	(969)
Later	16	29	11	5	14	4	10	10	99	(367)

Note:
Occupational groups are aggregates of the 24 Warwick Occupational Categories. See Furlong and Raffe (1989).

in the external labour market without acknowledging any help from YTS (22 per cent).

Consequences of YTS

What were the consequences for YTS trainees of leaving their schemes in these different ways? Table 4.4 summarizes some of these by reporting the percentages of YTS trainees respectively completing their YTS scheme, gaining qualifications from YTS (other than the YTS certificate), being still in a full-time job in autumn 1987, being still in the same occupational group as their YTS scheme, and receiving further employment-based training.

The first two consequences refer directly to the YTS experience itself. Internal recruits were more likely than external recruits to have completed their schemes; they were also more likely to have gained qualifications from YTS. These two consequences were correlated but by no means perfectly: some three-quarters of trainees with qualifications from YTS had National Certificate modules, which could be accumulated as trainees progressed through the scheme rather than awarded as a single group certificate on its completion (SED, 1983; Raffe, 1988d). Thus, among the internal recruits, 37 per cent even of those who had not completed their schemes reported some qualifications from YTS. Among the external recruits those helped by the 'content' of YTS were most likely, and those not acknowledging any help from YTS were least likely, to have qualifications from YTS.

Regardless of whether they had completed their schemes, more internal recruits than external recruits were still in full-time jobs in 1987. Among the external recruits those who had been helped by the content of YTS had the highest employment rate, at 77 per cent. (Of the remaining 23 per cent, 19 per cent were unemployed or on schemes; the others had left the full-time labour market.) More of those helped by content than of the other external recruits continued in the same occupation, but once again the proportion doing so (47 per cent) was well below those of the internal recruits (67 per cent and 71 per cent). More of the internal recruits had received employment-based training since leaving their schemes.

Table 4.4 shows figures for males and females combined. The separate male and female figures show the same direction of difference between internal and external recruits on all five measures, but a smaller difference for females

Table 4.4: Consequences of YTS, by YTS leaving profile

	% completed scheme	% with qualifications from YTS (1)	If in FT job in 1987			
			% in FT job in 1987	% in same occupation as YTS (2)	% reporting employment-based training since YTS (3)	(n)
Internal recruitment:						
before completing scheme	0	37	88	67	42	(158)
on completing scheme	100	58	88	71	53	(332)
External recruitment helped by:						
content of YTS	59	45	77	47	25	(158)
context of YTS	52	36	61	37	29	(74)
not helped by YTS	43	27	73	16	13	(250)
not known	29	35	66	18	22	(44)
Unemployment, no FT job						
by 1987	57	32	0	—	—	(199)
Others	54	37	37	35	13	(121)
All	58	40	62	49	34	(1336)

Notes:
1 Qualifications from YTS: excluding YTS certificate.
2 Same occupation: based on 24 Warwick Occupational Categories.
3 Employment-based training: any of day or block release at college, off-the-job training through work, on-the-job training at work.

than for males. For example, among males 92 per cent of all internal recruits were in full-time jobs in 1987 compared with only 70 per cent of all external recruits; the corresponding figures for females were 83 per cent and 74 per cent.

To summarize: internal recruits from YTS appear to have made smoother transitions to employment, and to have experienced greater continuity, than the external recruits. These are averaging statements which conceal wide variations, but it is striking that even among the external recruits those recruited on the basis of the content of YTS compared unfavourably with the internal recruits. There is little evidence that those not admitted by YTS to the (enterprise) internal labour market were helped to enter occupational labour markets of similar standing.

YTS and Recruitment to the Youth Labour Force

Further analyses, summarized here, examine the role of YTS in the training and recruitment of the 19-year-old workforce. Three quarters (75 per cent) of the year group were in the full-time labour market in autumn 1987, at around age 19. Nearly three quarters of these (55 per cent of the year group) were in full-time employment. Nearly half (47 per cent) of the full-time employees had at least started a YTS scheme, but only 24 per cent had been on YTS schemes in the same occupation (Warwick Occupational Category) as their current employment. Similar proportions of male and female employees had been on a YTS scheme in the same occupation as their current job, but many more males than females had been on a YTS scheme in a different occupation from their current job.

Occupational groups varied in the proportion of employees who had been on YTS, from 28 per cent (professional managerial and related) to 59 per cent (operatives and labourers). But they varied much more in the proportion who had been on YTS in the same occupation. Sales, craft and skilled manual, and clerical and secretarial workers were most likely to have been on YTS schemes in the same occupational group, and except for sales were unlikely to have been on YTS schemes in other occupational groups. Of the more detailed occupational categories, the highest proportion of former YTS trainees was found in construction craft occupations, 69 per cent of whose workers had been on YTS. This also had the highest proportion who had been on YTS in the same occupational category (54 per cent).

Only 30 per cent of all current full-time employees were 'direct' recruits from YTS to their current jobs. 'Direct' recruits include those who experienced unemployment between YTS and their current job, but exclude those who had left the full-time labour market for a spell after their scheme or who had changed jobs since YTS. More than half of these (17 per cent) had been recruited internally; 13 per cent had been recruited externally. Only 4 per cent of employees had been recruited directly to their current jobs on the basis of the content of their YTS schemes. This proportion was consistently low across occupations, not exceeding 5 per cent for any of the broader occupational groups (as shown in Table 4.3). Even among the twenty-four more detailed occupational categories the highest proportion was only 9 per cent (for secretarial occupations). On this evidence, the 'content' of YTS played a very small direct role in the recruitment and selection of the 19-year-old workforce, and there were no significant occupational labour markets in which its role was substantially greater.

Summary and Discussion

The question asked at the beginning of this paper was: to what extent do young people find jobs in the external labour market on the strength of the content of YTS? If we take respondents' accounts at face value, we conclude that only 11 per cent of trainees entered the external labour market on leaving their scheme and found full-time jobs on the basis of the scheme's content; and only 4 per cent of 19-year-old full-time employees had been recruited directly to their present jobs through the external labour market on the strength of the content of YTS schemes.

The transition from YTS to work was in many respects smoother and more continuous for the internal recruits. They were more likely to complete their schemes, more likely to move directly from YTS to employment, more likely to remain in full-time employment having found it, more likely to remain in the particular jobs they entered after YTS, more likely to remain in the same occupations as their YTS schemes, and more likely to receive further training. Although the trainees who found jobs helped by the content of YTS fared 'better' on most of these outcomes than other external recruits, they still compared unfavourably with the internal recruits.

All of these patterns varied with respect to gender, school qualification level, date of entry to the labour market and occupation. I have not attempted in this paper to tease out the separate influences of gender and occupation on the process of leaving YTS: in a highly gendered labour market this could be a rather fruitless, chicken-and-egg exercise. There was a tendency for YTS training to have more currency in the external market for females and female occupations than for males and male occupations, but the difference was only one of degree. The analysis failed to discover occupational areas where recruitment was dominated by the content of YTS sold in the external labour market. YTS may have offered indirect access to occupational labour markets, through providing access to apprenticeships which in turn gave entry to occupational labour markets (Marsden and Ryan, 1988); construction craft occupations are the most likely instance of this. But the analysis provides no evidence of occupational labour markets to which YTS was both a significant and a sufficient means of access.

These conclusions describe the one-year scheme. Comparisons within the sample do not suggest that the spread of certification on the two-year scheme will, on its own, dramatically enhance its external marketability. The increased length of training, and the greater emphasis on occupational skills, may have more effect. However if this were achieved at the expense of breadth the victory would be hollow. I return to this point later.

Does any of this matter? Even if YTS is primarily associated with a pattern of training for the internal labour market, does it not also seek to redress the imbalances associated with this pattern? Training for the internal market tends to be under-supplied (especially by smaller firms who fear poaching); but YTS seeks to compensate for this through the subsidy that it provides. Training for the internal market tends to be too narrow and specific, since firms do not wish to invest in skills that may be taken elsewhere; but YTS seeks to prevent this through a design framework that insists on a 'general' element.

There are at least two reasons why YTS' bias towards the internal labour market, and its apparently poor external marketability, may matter. The first is pragmatic. YTS needs to protect its position in a youth labour market characterized by growing supply shortages, at least in some areas, particularly of well qualified young people. To do this it needs to encourage more employers to use it as a way of recruiting and training their future workforce. But supply and demand are interdependent: one of the strongest disincentives to employers is the fear that YTS may not — or may no longer — attract young recruits of the calibre they seek. If the number of employers recruiting through YTS is to be maintained or increased, therefore, 'good' young workers must be willing to enter a YTS scheme in preference to an equivalent opening with a similar employer outside YTS. YTS must offer something extra — most plausibly, it must offer training with visible currency in the external labour market.

The second reason why all this matters is more fundamental. YTS aims to be an employer-led scheme that provides general and transferable training, suited to the more versatile workforce of the future. Its apparent failure to sell in the external labour market would seem to be a poor endorsement of the training and in particular of its general and transferable elements. The question arises, however, of whether the problem lies mainly in the failure of YTS to produce the necessary skills to the required standard, or in the failure of the British youth labour market to recognize and make use of the skills that are provided. In pursuing this question we must bear in mind that the data presented above refer to one-year YTS, whose main emphasis was on relatively general foundation skills.

Recent studies have drawn attention to the low levels and poor standards of vocational education and training in Britain compared to most of her industrial competitors (IMS, 1984; OECD, 1985; Prais and Wagner, 1983; Steedman, 1988; White, 1988). An influential and persuasive analysis sees Britain as 'trapped in a low-skills equilibrium, in which the majority of enterprises staffed by poorly trained managers and workers produce low-quality goods and services' (Finegold and Soskice, 1988, p. 22). The equilibrium is maintained by a 'self-reinforcing network of societal and state institutions which interact to stifle the demand for improvements in skill levels'. These institutions include 'the organization of industry, firms and the work process, the industrial relations system, financial markets, the state and political structure, as well as the operation of the ET (education and training) system'.

This analysis points to two possible interpretations of the findings of this paper. Given the diversity of YTS schemes, both may be valid to some extent.

The first interpretation sees YTS, and especially the one-year scheme, as part of the problem. The skills it produces are at too low a level, the training too rudimentary and under-resourced. The organization and funding of the scheme inhibits a substantial investment in quality training for the external labour market (Lee *et al.*, 1990); and 'the government's deregulatory enthusiasm' prevents the regulation that is required if effective occupational labour markets, and occupational training, are to be established (Marsden and Ryan, 1988, p. 14). The contribution of YTS, in this view, is doubly insidious. On the one hand, the quality of YTS training is low. On the other hand the *context* of YTS, at least of the higher-status schemes, is nevertheless favourable (that is, it provides routes to desired employment); and YTS therefore attracts well-qualified 16-year-olds away from the full-time education which would better serve their and the economy's long-term interests.

The second interpretation sees YTS as more sinned against than sinning. The pathology of the low-skills equilibrium, in this view, is not that employers fail to use or demand skills. There are, after all, several areas of skill shortage reported by employers themselves (TA, 1988). The problem is rather that their notions of skill and competence are narrow. They are narrow in the sense of being both enterprise- and occupationally-specific. Not only do employers prefer to train young people in the firm's own ways (Roberts, Dench and Richardson, 1987, p. 46) but they perceive as 'irrelevancies' attempts to develop knowledge and competences that are broader than those required by a single occupation (*ibid.*, p. 58). When employers recruit young workers they attach little weight to broadly-based vocational curricula or qualifications as criteria for selection (Bell *et al.*, 1988; Raffe, 1988d). They prefer to recruit at 16 and train (if at all) in their own ways. YTS falls foul of this syndrome because it attempts to develop broadly-based skills. At best it can 'go with the grain of the British youth labour market' by encouraging internal recruitment (Raffe, 1988c, p. 120). In this view analyses which define skill shortages solely in terms of traditional narrow concepts of skill (e.g. Deakin and Pratten, 1987) miss the real problem. They may even make it worse by reinforcing those definitions.

Other symptoms of this malaise include Britain's chronically low participation in full-time education beyond 16, the failure of employers to recognize and support the general vocational education provided through initiatives such as TVEI, and the lack of a strong full-time technical sector in British education. In this view one of the main dangers is that YTS may improve its marketability precisely by accommodating demands based on these narrow definitions of skill. Beset by economic and demographic pressures, and shackled by political constraints and the expectation that it be 'flexible' and 'industry-led', YTS may abandon any effort to introduce a broader concept of

71

vocational education and training of the kind that Britain's competitors have come to take for granted.

Acknowledgments

Work on this chapter was carried out as part of the project on Young People's Routes Into and Within the Labour Market, funded by the Industry Department for Scotland. The help of Andy Furlong and Peter Ritchie, my colleagues on the project, is gratefully acknowledged. David Finegold, Andy Furlong, Paul Ryan, Graham Senior and Hilary Steedman made helpful comments on earlier drafts, as did participants at the 1989 BSA Conference where the paper was first presented. The judgments and opinions expressed in this chapter are my own and are not necessarily shared by the Department or individuals mentioned above.

Chapter 5

Trainers and Tutors in the YTS Environment

Ken Parsons

The one year Youth Training Scheme launched in 1983 — which was increased to two years in 1986 — marked an important departure from previous job creation initiatives insofar as it provided an off-the-job educational element for each trainee for a minimum of twenty weeks over the two year period. The off-the-job (OJT) element was designed to complement the on-the-job work experience in such a way as to lead to a range of educational qualifications — some established, but many of them new ones. In this way education and work experience were to be integrated.

The off-the-job training was organized like the YTS itself around a range of 'occupational families', and the Managing Agents could either provide this themselves if they had the facilities (usually the case in larger companies), or they could rent the services of one of the growing numbers of private training centres or those of the local Further Education College. The MSC, now the Training Agency (TA), also provided curriculum guidelines and suggestions for the off-the-job training element and these were designed to introduce the trainee to aspects of the theory behind their occupational area, basic literacy and numeracy skills where required, as well as 'social and life skills'. The latter element could include interviewing skills which were thought to be lacking. The only thing explicitly forbidden was any political education.

These various elements of training were put together in such a way as to enhance the human capital of trainees in a 'profile': that is, a record of their achievements in and out of work, which was recorded in negotiation with a YTS tutor, as an individual testimony, thus helping to increase the confidence of the trainee and provide a source of information for employers.

However, since the Scheme was introduced rapidly and then frequently reorganized, the curriculum was often not well thought out or well tested and this allowed scope for interpretation by trainers. Thus the off-the-job element of the Youth Training Scheme poses some interesting problems. On the one hand it is part of a vocational training system, narrowly defined as equipping young people with specific skills for specific jobs, but on the other hand it is also supposed to provide — in a fairly limited way — an 'education for life'.

This development of the 'new vocationalism' occupying a new social terrain somewhere between work and education becomes particularly problematic with regard to the off-the-job training: here, the contradictions between educational and vocational philosophies are particularly acutely posed. The Government's preference for the dominance of the latter over the former is reflected in the encouragement of the use of private training centres over Further Education Colleges — the traditional provider of vocational education. However, many of the trainers working within the apparatus of the TA still prefer a broader interpretation of education. The trainer is at the sharp end of the YTS, theirs is the job of actually carrying it out.

The TA and YTS should not be seen as monolithic institutions; rather, they encompass a range of people at different levels with a range of interpretations of their roles. The 'official ideology' is that young people are being trained to improve the quality of their own skills and those of the British labour force in general. The off-the-job element should thus provide back-up for skills training as well as improving the 'employability' of trainees more generally. In the rhetoric surrounding the Scheme the Government has justified the investment of billions of pounds in order to solve the problems of youth unemployment and compensate for the alleged deficiences of the education system in turning out unemployable youths. This 'official ideology' was further reinforced in a multi-million pound advertising campaign, glossy brochures and much needed hype.

However, within the Scheme itself there is also evidence of scepticism and the development of 'subversive' ideologies. Those who hold them have to find some compromise in training within the Scheme. For this reason it is important to consider the position of those who actually carry out the training.

Apart from the work of Edwards (1984) and more recently, the contributors to *Education, Training and the New Vocationalism* (Pollard *et al.*, 1988) there appears to be little research on the YTS at the level of educational practices and especially staff perspectives and orientations. Therefore, the purpose of this paper is to describe and analyze the 'lived experiences' of the

YTS staff who teach, train and monitor the trainees as they progress through the scheme. The YTS staff are involved in the implementation and reception of national policy decisions at local level. Thus we need to capture the relationships between what C. Wright Mills has termed the 'personal troubles' of the staff during this process and examine how they manifest themselves in their orientations towards the scheme, and towards the 'public issue' of the new vocationalism in general. It is necessary, therefore, to pay serious attention to people's consciousness, as Lodziak points out: ' . . . not for reasons of engaging in that self-righteous exercise of ideology detection, but for reasons of finding out the kinds of motivations people have, and what the basis of these motivations are' (1988, p. 13). We need, thus, to examine the 'common sense constructs' that the trainers use in order to explain these 'lived experiences'. It follows therefore that an examination of the trainers' perspectives helps us to understand how these trainers construct their realities and define situations. Obviously it is impossible to tell what a person 'really believes' or to tap an individual's 'true' perspectives and orientations. However, as Dean and Foote Whyte remind us:

> . . . no matter how objective an informant seems to be, the research point of view is: the informant's statement represents merely the perception of the informant, filtered and modified by his cognitive and emotional reactions and reported through his personal verbal usages (1978, p.179).

Nevertheless by continual interviewing and observation over the period of a year or so it is possible to get some idea of what Woods has called 'the constructs of meanings — that is at the heart of social life' (1983, p. 17).

From April 1987 to the summer of 1988 I traced a group of 150 YTS trainees and fifteen of their trainers/tutors as they progressed through the Scheme, using a combination of questionnaires, participant observation, group and individual interviews. It is the data generated from this latter method which forms the bulk of the information contained in this paper.

The Sample

The semi-structured tape-recorded interviews involved fifteen YTS staff at two off-the-job (OJT) training and educational establishments in Surfton. Surfton is a large city in the South West of England with over seventy YTS schemes in progress. The off-the-job training element can take the form of attendance at day release, block release (with one or more blocks) and/or residential periods varying according to the nature and requirements of individual schemes. The specific curriculum of the OJT element of YTS depends on the occupational training area where each trainee is situated. A range of training is offered, which included literacy, numeracy, computing, personal effectiveness and other vocationally orientated skills and qualifications.

The YTS is not uniform throughout. Each scheme may place more emphasis on 'social', 'training' or 'educational' aspects of the curriculum, or attention may be focused more directly at the 'work ethic'. Scheme staff may come from a variety of industrial backgrounds bringing different orientations to the scheme. The fifteen trainers interviewed consisted of nine females and six males, two of whom were aged in their twenties, eight in their thirties, three in their forties and two in their fifties. Although during the course of my reasearch I contacted over forty YTS trainers, these particular fifteen were interviewed in more detail because they were directly associated with the 150 trainees who form part of the overall research. The majority had previous experience of employment which related to the trainees' occupational areas. A total of six possessed either a degree or teaching certificate. The remaining nine could be said to have personal histories of a practical nature, with only a minority holding a teaching qualification such as the In-service Youth Trainers Award. Over half had taught on other prevocational courses, such as the Certificate of Pre-Vocational Education (CPVE) or the Youth Opportunities Programme (YOP), whilst several had taught in schools or on traditional apprenticeship courses. In general, three trainers had fourteen to twenty-five years of teaching experience, eight had three to ten years and four had less than one year.

The YTS tutor, whilst crucial to the quality of training provided, is in a very precarious occupational position. They are mostly employed on temporary contracts which last as long as the scheme will last and this is itself uncertain with booms and slumps in the labour market and political favour or disfavour for the Scheme being somewhat volatile (Ainley and Corney, 1990). Whilst some may hold teacher training qualifications, the tendency has been to avoid the creation of a professionally qualified stratum of trainers (Davies, 1986). Consequently, there is little uniformity in the character of trainers and they carry out a low paid, highly stressful job coping with very high numbers of trainees — some of them truculent and resistant to the idea of sitting at a desk for any period of time after they have just escaped from school. In addition, their organization — and their job with it — could be dissolved at any moment.

Before the trainers' perspectives are examined it is important to provide a formal description of the two schemes in which they work, because the different organizational structures within each scheme have important effects on the trainers' ability to act on their perspectives.

Scheme Organization

The first scheme is situated at the Danby Centre Ltd, which is a Managing Agency approved by the Training Agency to provide training schemes in the retail and distributive industries, and which offers over twenty retail outlets to trainees. The Danby Centre is responsible for sixty-one trainees at every level of the scheme. The five staff work as a team and their main duties include scheme advertising and recruitment, providing trainees with work experience on employers' premises (on-the-job) and catering for the off-the-job training (OJT) and educational component which takes place at the centre itself. They also act as personal assessors to the trainees which involves monitoring the quality of training, the appropriate integration between on- and off-the-job training, the trainees' working conditions and their general welfare as they progress through the scheme.

The second OJT location is situated at the local further education college's Marton Annexe. The remaining ten YTS trainers were interviewed here. Again the criteria for selection was their direct involvement with eighty-nine of the remaining 150 trainees involved in the research. Originally the further education college functioned as its own Managing Agent and had the same monitoring duties as the Danby Centre. However, after the summer of 1987, the County Council which funds the college, handed the role of managing agent over to South West Skills which is one of four major managing agents covering the majority of occupational areas, including 'social care', 'clerical', 'catering' and 'building and construction' and these formed the remaining occupational areas chosen for the research. This resulted in South West Skills deciding to fund the college for the off-the-job training element only, thus reducing the duties of the college staff, including the ten interviewed, considerably. Unlike in the Danby Centre they had lost control of coordinating the scheme. The situation was further compounded by South West Skills — which was a relatively new entity — experiencing 'teething problems' in organizing, implementing and coordinating schemes, and by structural changes in the Scheme itself during the summer of 1988.

Two models of organization emerged: the Danby Centre was able to maintain more regular contact and monitoring of their trainees, being more comprehensively responsible for the overall organization of the scheme itself; whilst the Marton Annexe has had its trainee contact and monitoring duties restricted — the tutor services were hired for the off-the-job training element only.

Trainer Perspectives

What emerges from the data on the trainers' perspectives is that although they may have different understandings with regard to the functions of YTS and their role within the process, it is apparent that two general perspectives do appear. Elaborating on similar models to those of Rosie (1988) these perspectives can be categorized as a 'Needs of Production Model' (NOP) and a 'Holistic Model'.

The characteristics of the NOP model consist of trainers whose approach towards training and education is didactic; thus they see their main role as equipping the trainees with the appropriate skills necessary for the needs of production. They are much more receptive towards official discourses as to the purpose of the scheme which are expounded by the MSC/TA, the Government and the media.

The holistic perspective consists of a heuristic approach towards education and training; thus the trainees are encouraged to learn things for themselves — it is a more trainee-centred approach. Trainers who hold this perspective may be critical towards the general philosophy of YTS and of the new vocationalism — their views may, therefore, be subversive to the 'official ideology' of the TA. They identify wider social influences on their role within the framework of the scheme and hold a much more liberal approach towards the scheme and social life in general.

These two levels of trainer perspectives lead to two different sets of orientations towards the Scheme and their 'lived experiences' within it. The speech used by the trainers in order to describe and account for their lived experiences can be aligned with Giddens' (1976) discussion of consciousness in which he distinguishes the unconscious from two modes of consciousness: practical consciousness and discursive consciousness. Practical consciousness is defined in terms of 'tacit stocks of knowledge which actors draw upon in the construction of social activity', whereas discursive consciousness involves 'knowledge which actors are able to express on the level of discourse'.

If we apply these concepts to the YTS trainers, it will be seen that those perspectives which reflect the holistic model are more likely to describe and account for thier orientations by using elaborated discourses to express themselves — or in other words they use discursive consciousness. Some of the speech elements described in Cole's (1984) study of 'school teacher consciousness' can be used here as evidence of discursive consciousness. For example, holistic trainers tend to introduce abstract concepts, rather than focusing on just particular concrete events. They tend to offer extended explanations of their observations as opposed to normative evaluations. They are also inclined to reveal scepticism and a willingness to tolerate ambiguity rather than a dogmatic certainty that tends to accompany normative evaluation.

Those trainers whose perspectives align themselves with a NOP model use a more restricted discourse and reflect much more established attitudes in orientations towards the Scheme and to society in general. Therefore, they tend to express 'taken for granted', 'common sense', 'that's the way it's done' type of perspectives. Furthermore, within the Danby Centre and the Marton Annexe both the NOP and the holistic models exist.

In general, then, these two trainer perspectives were reflected in their orientations towards the Scheme, the politics surrounding the new vocationalism, their relationship with the MSC/TA, Managing Agents, employers and trainees as well as in their own teaching.

Trainer Perspectives and the New Vocationalism

The trainers' general aims and objectives towards the trainees and the new vocationalism now need to be outlined in order to demonstrate more fully the characteristics of these two perspectives. If we examine the NOP perspectives and their orientations, the interview data shows that they considered their main duty as being able to equip the young person with what they perceived to be the necessary social etiquette needed for the labour market.

They thus regard personal development, teamwork and confidence-building skills as essential aids to achieve this goal. The following quote is a typical example from John, a catering trainer at Marton Annexe:

> They have probably spent the last three years at school, skiving off so we have to persuade them, usually by docking their pay, that they have to come in every day and be clean and hygienic. They have to relate to other people in the class and at work. We've had two people this year who have been dismissed. They couldn't relate to others, they had to go eventually . . . They've got to have the attitude that they've got to be responsible for their own futures and that they can't live off the Government for the rest of their lives.

On the other hand, trainers who hold a holisitic perspective are more likely to have aims and objectives which reflect a trainee-centred approach. They do see the importance of 'personal development skills', but they also see that many trainees have systematically 'failed' whilst at school and that trainee participation on the Scheme comes at the end of a long process rather than the beginning of a short experience.

The following comment is from Christine, a social care trainer also at Marton's, who is a qualified school teacher with fourteen years' teaching experience:

> The main objectives I feel are for these youngsters to reach their full potential. It sounds a bit high flown, but I try and give them as many opportunites to reach that potential as is possible . . . they have not opened their mouths since they left junior school . . . em . . . in primary schools and junior schools education is very much child-centred and the teacher plans the curriculum for each child. They go to secondary school *en masse* and I may be biased but I think that secondary schools are organized for those 10 per cent of pupils who might go on to higher education. They're very much geared to GCE as it was. So the type of youngster I get has been wasted from 11 to 16. They come to me with great resentment, they hated school and weren't allowed any choice or say in what happened to them, they were told they were failures. I mean the usual thing if you go around

the table when they first come in and say 'tell me one thing about yourself' — they say 'thick', 'can't do it', 'stupid', all the time.

This holistic perspective can be seen also in the trainers' conceptions of their trainees, as they tended to describe them as 'young adults' with 'separate individual needs', emphasizing for some 'training' and 'educational' elements, whilst for others the focus might be on the 'social' aspect of the Scheme. NOP trainers, however, were more likely to see their trainees as 'young workers' or as 'born carpenters or chefs' who therefore, needed skills in specific forms of work.

All the trainers agreed that vocational preparation courses, whether they be in or out of school, were 'here to stay'. However, those trainers who held a NOP perspective were more likely to see the state's role in regard to young people's jobs, training and education as a necessary intervention in view of the present 'economic climate', whilst holistic trainers tended to have more pessimistic views as to the state's role in this process. The following dialogues with two retail trainers, at the Danby Centre, illustrate these diverse perspectives even in the same off-the-job training setting. The first conversation is with William who holds a NOP perspective.

KP   Could you tell me what your feelings are towards vocational training and educational courses?

William I think the state of the country means we haven't taken vocational training seriously over the years and I would make it compulsory for all young people to do some sort of training. I know that this is a political hot potato, but I would make it a law of the land that anyone leaving school at 16 had to go into some sort of training situation for three years ... I sometimes go back perhaps twenty-five to thirty years to the time when you had to pay to get trained. My friends went into apprenticeships and earned peanuts for years and don't forget also we had the spectre of National Service ... In the old world we would accept discipline, we used to accept what our parents told us and get on with it ... We're reluctant to accept basic discipline.

KP   What do you consider to be the cause of this slip in standards?

William I don't know. I mean it's an interesting argument ... em ... I don't know, independence perhaps, the 'why should I get out of bed and go to work?' kind of attitude. Maybe we've been a bit too liberal with the social security over the last twenty or thirty years. I believe in social security but maybe the people who claim it aren't vetted closely enough, you know, maybe ... er ... or maybe people have too many children and can't discipline them.

The same initial question was put to Sally, who heads the team of retail trainers at the Danby Centre, and demonstrates a holistic perspective.

KP   Could you tell me what your feelings are towards vocational training and educational courses?

Sally Well it depends what you think education is about. I mean, I don't think human beings were intended to go down into the earth and scrabble about for coal, or do all these awful jobs that people do ... Many of the teachers I meet don't think that vocational training is important. Teachers are fighting tooth and nail to keep their industry intact and they are not going to succeed, not with this present Government. Because the intention now is to train youngsters as workers, I see my role as being put into a situation and try to do my best for the youngsters and try and prevent them from being abused. .... skills training establishments should open to anybody so that if you were 10 years old and wanted to learn about a computer you would go in and get specialized about that and if you were 70 years old you would go in the same day as well ... My aim would be to have a group in here of fifteen people in retailing but they would be at all sorts of levels. I find this much more rewarding and it would take care of the problems that a lot of people or staff have, with trainee behaviour.

KP   If you could change anything about this process, then what would it be?

Sally Well, I suppose you're talking about YTS but my own view is that they shouldn't have such things as school anyway. I don't like segregating people and putting them into institutions from an early age — I think it's appalling, I don't like schools.

KP   Do you ever express these political views to your trainees?

Sally   I have never put across any political viewpoint. I've never felt that I
       would be happy to do so. I'm not sure how my own political bias,
       which is a minority one in this country, would come through. So I
       really don't feel justified in doing that, and in this particular
       area . . . geographically . . . the youngsters when they first start are
       extremely Conservative. I mean, they are more right of Thatcher
       than she is. So it's extremely difficult for me, you know, I would
       need about ten years of political education with them to try and
       change them or raise their consciousness or whatever . . . Besides, I
       don't think you learn politics this way anyway, I mean, it comes to
       you through your pores — doesn't it?

It can be seen from these two dialogues that on the one hand William (NOP) is
more inclined than Sally (holistic) to align himself with the many
conventional, popular notions and 'moral panics' associated with the young
working-class unemployed (see Cohen, 1972, for a discussion of this).
Therefore, he tends to individualize the rapid changes in the economy by
focusing on the trainees and their parents. However, on the other hand, Sally is
much more critical of the social and political context where schooling,
education and training take place, offering her own remedies to improve this
general learning environment.

Let us now examine the two perspectives as expressed within different organizational contexts — the Danby Centre and Marton Annexe.

Trainer Perspectives and Organizational Contexts

One of the major problems associated with the Scheme nationally and locally is
the integration between on-the-job and off-the-job elements, which can lead to
a mis-match of trainee placements. For the Danby Centre, even with its more
enabling structure, this was a difficult goal to strive for and called for
improvization upon the national programme package that they were required
to adhere to because, as one trainer commented, 'the trainees and employers do
not understand the obscure instructions'. However, the constraining structure
of the Marton Annexe made this problem even more difficult to monitor and
on occasions impossible to alleviate.

The following dialogues provide contrasting trainer perspectives on this problem. The first, again, is from Sally at the Danby Centre, who holds a holistic perspective.

KP   In your opinion are the skills that the trainees learn on their off-the-job training integrated to their on-the-job training?

Sally   There is a problem with integration. It's very difficult, I have a view that when the trainees are here with us at the centre then they are not being abused at their work experience placements, or that being here helps to compensate for some of the integration problems... In a way I see off-the-job as a safeguard for the youngsters, although that's not how others see it obviously.

KP   The MSC do spend a lot of money on the Scheme, so why do you think these integration and general scheme problems still exist?

Sally   I think really because the MSC has failed as the quango that they are. They've failed to control it . . . to organize it properly. Their attitude from the beginning is one of 'Well, you do it and we'll tell you if it's right'. They don't know what they want so they are hoping that you will actually tell them. Anyone who comes up with an idea, they think 'Oh yes, that fits in nicely so we'll fund that and we'll see in the end if it's any good'. Meanwhile all these little guinea pigs [trainees] have been on that course or on the receiving end.

The same initial question was now put to Peter who teaches at the Marton Annexe on the Building and Construction course and whose views reflect the general position of NOP trainers.

KP   In your opinion are the skills that the trainees learn on their off-the-job training integrated to their on-the-job training?

Peter   No

KP   Why not?

Peter   Well we've had a lot of mixed students in the way of trades, and . . . er . . . well a lot of them shouldn't be on this course. For example, we have painting and decorating trainees, when this is a building and construction course, so how could anyone possibly say that this is integrated?

KP   South West Skills has placed these trainees with you?

Peter   Oh yes, but it's just the case of keeping them occupied . . . I think, I could be wrong, it's only my opinion. I mean we had one girl who wanted to do just bricklaying and she left after ten weeks because we simply weren't covering aspects of the course she needed to learn. It's rather like taking somebody who wants to be a violinist and train them to play a trombone or something, it's quite ridiculous.

KP   Do you see these lack of integration problems as being due to the management of South West Skills?

Peter   Well . . . (laughs) . . . with a new entity they're just getting their act together, or trying to. Before South West Skills took over, Marton's were a very good system, they had the training where the whole system operated around the student. I think the MAs [managing agents] go out and sell X number of students with . . . to me . . . not very much thought and put them into various occupations and I think before the students decide on an occupation you should spend a lot more time talking to the students and discover what their background is in order so that they can make a better choice.

It can be seen that Sally has a holistic perspective towards scheme organizational problems and expresses herself in a discursive consciousness mode. For example, she sees off-the-job training as providing the trainees with a safety-net which will compensate for the scheme problems associated with the work-experience placement. Further discussions with, and observations of, Sally demonstrated that she not only sees the value of off-the-job training as providing the trainees with the opportunity of studying for vocational certificates but she had also worked at winning the space within the formal framework of off-the-job training which reflected her holistic perspectives and orientations. However, Peter can be seen to reflect his NOP perspective with the appropriate practical consciousness mode of expression. Although he identifies the same scheme organizational problems as Sally, his main concern is that these problems interfere with his role of equipping the trainees with the skills necessary for the labour market. Sally and Peter — indeed, all fifteen trainers — had redefined their formal roles at grassroot levels, which gave them different levels of relative autonomy which in turn reflected the appropriate holistic or NOP paradigms. These roles had been somewhat compounded for the ten Marton staff because, due to South West Skills taking over the role of Managing Agents, the space provided for this relative autonomy had been restricted.

However, the space that all the trainers had won was often won for different reasons depending on the particular perspectives that the trainers had. The participant observation aspect of the research serves to illustrate this point. A selection of trainers and their trainees were observed in their off-the-job classrooms and workshop settings. Although often reflecting traditional school environments, many of these sessions consisted of a much more relaxed atmosphere. At times they took on the appearances of a 'youth club' where trainee activity was often boisterous and centred around bopping to music, sexual flirtations, and horseplay. Male trainees would often swagger around the room, macho style, whilst the different dress, style and demeanour between the two sexes would be quite prominent. During this process trainee talk tended to centre around sexual activities, courtship and marriage, family and friends, going to the pub or music and fashion.

The trainers' activity in these settings would often reflect the survival strategies described by Woods' (1983) study of school teachers. Such strategies as 'negotiation' (you play ball with me and I'll play ball with you), 'fraternization' (if you can't beat them, join them) or 'humour' and 'jokes' would often be employed.

When asked to account for these trainee activities a typical feeling amongst holistic trainers was reflected by Pam at the Danby Centre:

> ... when we first started we had arm chairs, now we have desks and chairs, so it's a bit more formal but we do try to keep the youth club atmosphere ... Most youngsters who come to YTS have had enough of school, they don't want to stay on and take further qualifications, not necessarily because they're not 'bright' because they are 'bright', they just hated school and being identified with those sorts of controls really ... The music is a great help and when

they do talk about 'marriage', 'courtship' and 'going to the pub' well it allows them to relax from the work experience.

NOP trainers see this process in a very different light, as Emily, a clerical trainer from Marton's, demonstrates:

> The fact that they talk while they are working, well that is part of our policy, because if you're at work you talk to your mates about what you did last night, what you saw on television, etc. It's got to be controlled though, it depends on what the trainees are doing . . . I try to be, in a way, an office supervisor, rather than a teacher. Our job really isn't teaching. I mean you can't have them doing a knees up in the middle of the room any more than you could have them talking when they should be learning, but that is another part of their training. They have to learn when they can do these things.

The point here is that for holistic trainers (as indicated earlier by Sally) these 'youth club' orientated sessions can be seen, in the main, as an arena whereby the trainees are able to forget their previous experiences of school whilst at the same time allowing them to 'recharge their batteries' after the rigours of their work-experience placements. NOP trainers, however, tended to see this process as mirroring some of the activities associated with the workplace, with their own role reflecting that of a works' supervisor.

Even on occasions when NOP trainers were more critical of the Scheme (as Peter indicated earlier) the reason tended to be because the targets of their criticism interfered with their NOP perspectives and orientations. This can be demonstrated further by focusing on one such criticism — the profiling process. This is a report which logs the trainees' progress during their participation on the Scheme. The following dialogues are with three trainers: Christine (social care — holistic), Peter (Building Trades — NOP) and William (Retail — NOP).

KP   Profiling is a central part of YTS schemes. What are your general feelings about it?

Christine Well . . . I try and look at them every week that they are in, but the great difficulty with formal profiles are that you miss a lot of things. These youngsters are able and er . . . er . . . crafty enough and worldly wise, street wise . . . enough not to put it in writing what they feel and very often on my assessment sheets they have to write what they feel and they say 'What shall I write, Christine?', and I say 'If you want to write a load of crap then write it — you can say what you like' . . . and I leave them alone to write it on their own and I don't get that, even from a youngster that I know would like to write 'this is a load of crap'. I get 'I have enjoyed the course very much' . . . (laughs). So anything in writing they don't want to know. My attitude towards written profiles reads slightly different to Managing Agents' or other lecturers' that you meet. I find very little value in writing . . . everybody wants things in writing, everybody wants proof. Now I don't want proof of a youngster's work, it's in my brain and their brain, it's in their emotions and you know, it's abstract . . . I mean what I assess on is their opinions, there, when we sit together, one to one for assessment, well it's a very artificial situation, obviously, because they're called in one by one, I try and do it as informally as possible but I can't do it all the time. I want to see them, how they grow, how they would cope in a particular situation, that to me is a profile.

Peter (NOP) offered the following response to the same initial question:

Peter   Well I'm not sure about the log books, I wonder how many employers will say 'Oh we must have a look at your log book and see what's written down in there', but when it boils down to it, it boils down to whether or not they can do the job. I mean, they may start a job on say a three month trial and if they can do it then it doesn't matter what their blinking log book says, if they can do it, if they can produce good work then you've got a job . . . I mean, one of the things on the profiles is that you don't put anything negative, it all has to be positive. Well to me this is a misguided way of trying to boost them, but it doesn't because profiles are a con. I'll tell them verbally that they've done a job wrong . . . er . . . building a wall or whatever, I'll say 'That is crap' and they'll appreciate that. Also when they've done a good job you say 'That's bloody good, you've done a bloody good job'.

Whilst William, also NOP, suggests that:

> profiling is a good idea but I think we've gone over the top with all
> the recording systems now...we seem to do profiling
> and...em...listing and writing and things like that for listing
> and profiling's sake now...it's, I mean, if you've got a person in a
> placement who is doing well and who is obviously improving and
> is happy, but is very reluctant to fill his/her log book as you want
> them to do, well what decision do you make?...I'd be very
> reluctant to boot anyone off the Scheme who didn't write their
> reports or fill in a personal effectiveness report enough...we tend
> to do things two or three times. I think, for instance, the leaving
> certificate is a bit crazy. You can be a brain surgeon and get one
> piece of paper and be on YTS and get the story of your life almost, I
> mean, it's crazy.

What the above dialogues show is that on the one hand it can be seen that
Christine is wary of attaching too much importance to profiles being used as
proof of a trainee's progress on the Scheme. Other methods of measuring a
trainee's ability must also be employed. For example, she sees the actual
'sitting down process' involved in profiling as being more beneficial for the
trainee as it provides an arena which allows for a healthy discussion to take
place between trainer and trainee. She is critical of the official purpose of a
profile but remedies this tension by adopting an heuristic approach towards her
trainees which allows for both parties to negotiate accepted levels of
assessment. Furthermore, Christine's holistic approach enables her to
appreciate the effects on the trainees of wider social influences.

On the other hand both Peter and William are critical of profiles, too, but
for different reasons. For example, Peter describes profiles as being a 'con', and
suggests that verbal information is more important in assessing a trainee's
progress than the written word, whilst William sees the amount of paperwork
involved as 'crazy' and 'over the top'. However, these comments are a
reflection of the NOP perspective because the targets of their criticisms —
profiles and paperwork — are seen as obstacles which restrict or interfere with
what they consider to be their prime duty, which is to equip the trainee for the
labour market and the needs of production.

It must be stressed here that trainer adherence to either perspective is not a rigid exercise — indeed, the generation of categories for any social data is a difficult process. The NOP and holistic perspectives do not exist in a vacuum as they are related to wider societal structures, including the characteristics of the social terrain. Therefore, the perspectives and the 'common sense' discourses of trainers take place in the context of economic conditions. Furthermore, when the trainers construct definitions they may be influenced by a range of factors within this social terrain. They could, for instance, employ 'cultural' definitions: that is, ones derived from their class and status group in a particuar geographical context. They could also employ 'habitual' definitions — ones derived from popular ideologies and the mass media. Finally they could also employ 'personal' definitions — ones derived from direct general experience which is to some extent unique. Their views are shaped not just by the way they see themselves but also by the way they think others perceive them and the way in which they attempt to conform to their perceived external normative standards. Thus, the different perspectives of the trainers are by no means free from the pressures of social institutions or the organization of particular off-the-job training centres.

Personal biography also plays a part. For example, Williamson's (1982) study of trainers on the Youth Opportunities Programme (YOP) highlights two general models of trainer perspectives which are related to their personal histories. The first model includes those individuals who can be described as having backgrounds of a professional, managerial or supervisory nature, such as graduates, teachers and social workers. They regard the main purpose of YOP as providing the trainees with educational and social skills, thus reducing the importance of learning specific work-based tasks. The second model consists of trainers from industrial working backgrounds who do not overemphasize the educational and social aspects of YOP, preferring instead to concentrate on offering training in specific forms of work.

The data obtained from my own research, although not permitting large scale generalizations due to the small number of informants, does in fact reflect many of the elements found in Williamson's study. In particular, cases of the more discursively conscious trainers (holistic) that I interviewed, in almost every instance, had participated in either degree studies — a PGCE, Cert. Ed or further education course — or had supervised young people in many different social settings. Therefore, these variables seem to be major factors with the holistic perspective.

Dealing with Individual Trainee Problems

Let us now examine one specific area where the trainers have been forced to create the appropriate space within the formal structure of OJT in order to accommodate trainee difficulties that they encounter. The official duties expected of YTS staff do require a certain amount of time being spent on the 'guidance', 'counselling' and 'general welfare' of trainees as they progress through the Scheme.

However, all fifteen trainers (and many more who were not systematically interviewed) suggested that they needed to devote 25 per cent of their time, effort and energies in dealing with 'individual trainee problems' which far exceeded their official duties. These extra-curricular activities and how the trainers coped with them were part of their 'lived experiences', and they became routinized events in their day-to-day working lives. Furthermore, all the trainees claimed that the MSC/TA would not 'take on board' these issues and did not recognize them as part of the formal curriculum of the Scheme.

The trainers encountered a vast array of individual trainee troubles, including emotional problems, family break-ups, homelessness, courtship difficulties, pregnancies, sexually transmitted diseases and so on. The majority of trainers regarded the regular occurrence of these problems as a new phenomenon in the late 1970s and 1980s. In order to deal with these difficulties the trainers described themselves as having to perform the role of a series of professionals, thus donning the hats of not only a trainer/teacher but also of amateur social worker, welfare officer, marriage guidance counsellor, youth and community worker, police officer or, more informally, friendly aunt/uncle or 'mother confessor'.

The following dialogues are with Sue (clerical) who holds a NOP perspective. This is followed by Simon (Building Trades) whose comments illustrate fully many of the most important characteristics of the holisitic perspective.

KP   Can you tell me what your feelings are towards the individual trainee problems that you encounter?

Sue   Oh yes, oh yes . . . (sights . . . laughs) . . . well, 16 and 17 is a very funny age. I deal mainly with girls here. They [the trainees] are either 'right up there' or 'right down there' in terms of their emotions. We seem to come across youngsters who don't seem to develop the right relationships with their parents. I'm not saying that it's totally the youngsters' fault because their parents are not educated enough . . . well to deal with those youngsters . . . So it's usually a crisis at home. It seems nowadays that it is easier for young people to just leave home. Things are made easier for them so they leave and then they get problems which stem from that as well.

KP   What do you think causes these individual trainee problems?

Sue   I've got a feeling that a lot of these problems do stem from unemployment, but I feel that a lot of them stem from trainees' parents. I don't feel that the parents assist young people in standing on their own two feet these days. Over the years we've become conditioned to expect a lot of things to be done for us . . . it's like kindly 'big brother', all these social service agencies. Therefore, the parents have stopped thinking things like 'Now what can we do to get out of this situation? They resent being in a situation and they say 'What is the Government going to do about it, what are "they" going to do?' and this attitude communicates itself to the young people. Parents often think that they have a wonderful child and it wasn't their child's fault that, say, they were kicked out of their work-experience placement or whatever.

Simon (holistic) offered the following comment to the same initial question:

. . . well . . . we deal with social problems from little things like the guy who is just unhygienic to the lad who has been battered by his parents, incest, or they will tell you quite openly about having babies and having abortions . . . Actually coming into that environment I found it really, really, not difficult, but staggering. The amount of youngsters who were out there having these problems.

Now of course I've come across vast other problems. I was amazed at the attitude problems and of the amount of kids who went to see psychiatrists because of their behavioural problems. I mean I was not prepared at all I was just, well you know — you learn very quickly you are chucked in at the deep end. You think

'Oh I'll teach these youngsters how to do painting and decorating' and you end up having to do a whole different training routine . . . the thing I've learnt about teaching especially with the premium trainees is that you've got to break down things and be very, very patient and let them discover things for themselves . . . don't be afraid to let the youngster make the mistake because that's the way they learn . . .

One of the biggest problems with premiums, well basics as well, is their low self-esteem. [The terms 'basic' and 'premium' refer to the MSC/TA trainee funding categories]. They've been told in their school and home environments that they're stupid, that they're not capable of doing a job of work. So what I've got to do is build those bricks up and say 'Look, you are capable'. Out there in society they're being told, say on the telly, all types of media, they're being told that if you come from a particular background then you are going to be stupid. Not in their consciousness, but subconsciously it's going on all the time, they are being battered and battered down and what our job is is to build them up.

KP   What do you think causes these individual trainee problems?

Simon   I think it's definitely a social problem. You go back to the family of youngsters and you'll see that often the parents are also from a bad family environment. So it's just a vicious circle.

On the one hand the reasons offered by Sue (NOP) in order to explain these individual trainee problems, are in terms of individual pathology. She implies that the main factor which affects the trainees' present and future prospects are their own or their parents' attitudes. Thus she tends to look for individual remedies to problems — by changing the attitudes of trainees and helping them to conform to society. On the other hand Simon (holistic) sees a trainee's class, home and school background as important factors which may cause these problems to occur — he sees the main problem as one of social deprivation. The young person's attitudes, rather than being a problem themselves, are seen as a fatalistic adaption to deprived social circumstances. He sees his role as compensating for economic and social oppression located externally to the classroom. Therefore, Simon locates individual trainee problems in the context of wider social structures.

Conclusion

Four main points emerge from the scenes sketched in this paper. First, that two key models of trainer perspectives — the 'Needs of Production' (NOP) and 'Holistic' — have been identified. Whilst all trainers may be critical of aspects of the Scheme the holistic perspective could be seen as forming part of an ideology subversive to 'official ideologies' within the YTS. Second, not only do the trainers experience different degrees of scheme complications, depending on the different organizational structures of each off-the-job training establishment, but they have worked at winning the space within this formal framework which allows them to participate in practices and activities which are not part of the official framework. Third, this unofficial space has been won for two reasons. On the one hand all the trainers have created their own autonomy in order to remedy or cope with the deficiencies associated with the formal framework — such as lack of integration between the on- and off-the-job training element. However, this autonomy has been won for different purposes reflecting either the NOP or holistic perspective. This is also the case when the trainers account for the problems associated with any 'space impingement' occurring due to the South West Skills takeover at the Marton Annexe, resulting in the curtailment of staff duties.

On the other hand, the trainers have been forced to create additional space which will allow them to cater for issues which are outside this official curriculum — such as 25 per cent of their time being spent on individual trainee problems. The fourth point is that the research suggests that although these individual trainee problems may be variously described by trainers as 'pathological' (in the case of NOP trainers) or 'social' (in the case of holistic trainers) they all see them as being on the increase in the late 1970s and 1980s. However, we can question whether this is the case; in the 1950s, 1960s and early 1970s the social terrain where young people's job training and education took place was different in character and there was not space to allow young people to discuss *their* lived experiences with adult tutors on a systematic basis. The issues raised in discussions between trainers and trainees should perhaps not be seen so much as 'problems', but rather this should be seen as an 'arena of confession' which has allowed young people to talk about their life histories and the social influences affecting them. What can be seen to have taken place is that over a period of one or two years the trainees have exposed their trainers to the 'rawness' of working-class life with all its ups and downs, its restricted life chances in gaining society's rewards. These are not necessarily seen as problems by trainees, they could be seen as accounts of what it is like to be growing up working-class in the 1980s.

Note

No assumption must be made in regard to the specific geographical location of the research, the training and educational establishments or the identity of those individuals involved.

Acknowledgments

I would like to thank the training staff and trainees at the Danby Centre and Marton Annexe for their help during the research. I am also grateful to Claire Wallace whose help has benefited this paper.

Chapter 6

Interpreting Vocationalism: Youth Training and Managerial Practices

Joan Chandler

Training in Britain has been approached by policy makers and economic planners as an ingredient in a rational economy where the needs of individuals and companies may be integrated and served, where training improves valued skills and where there is investment in people as human capital (Rist, 1986). In the post-war years training policy has been linked to a corporate state and a planned economy. Within this the voluntarism of employers' involvement in training was hardly compromised (Sheldrake and Vickerstaff, 1986). The Thatcher years have done much to dismantle the corporate state and the economy of Britain has been transformed by the reorganization of capitalism. Throughout this, training and vocationalism have reflected class interest and political expediency so that these are clear reference points in debates about YTS.

The current wave of youth training, developed as a response to youth unemployment and the grumblings of employers in recession, has sought to impose a training and enterprise culture on Britain. Youth training was part of a package of measures instituted under a wider programme of renewed vocationalism. Under the Manpower Services Commission (MSC) training was delivered through an agency structure, sub-contracted to employers and a motley collection of training organizations. MSC did not itself devise or run training programmes, but sub-contracted them to a wide assortment of bodies and individuals, organizations whose part in training could be expanded or contracted with each shift in policy. These managing agents of youth training have come to occupy a new position in British training history. They are funded partly by Government through the Training Agency and partly by employers through their contributions. They now control the entry of the majority of 16- to 17-year-olds into the labour market. Within this overall frame Government has reinterpreted the 'training problem' and restructured and reorganized its relationship with managing agencies. Recent changes have led YTS increasingly to serve the immediate interests of employers, to shed any involvement with the trade union movement, to be employer-led — and it is shortly to become employer-owned and controlled.

This paper is an exploration of the management practices of schemes in response to YTS2 and the day to day implications of these practices for vocationalism. Dale (1985b) has argued that new vocationalism does not go uncontested by the teachers and trainers, by administrators or by young people themselves, but there are issues aside from those of the contest. Jamieson and Lightfoot (1981) described the ambiguities of the school-industry movement and the complexity of an education programme designed to encourage children to learn about work. Within training schemes, which are closer to industry than schools, one might expect vocationalism to be more straightforward. However, the paper argues that it is not.

Firstly, the recent wave of new vocationalism developed with dual aims: to produce a more skilled and flexible workforce and to soak up the young unemployed and keep them receptive and ready for possible work later. Differences between managing agencies mixed with the dual aims of YTS to create a dichotomous structure of schemes under YTS1. Mode A schemes were run by employers or private training agencies and training took place on employers' premises, while Mode B schemes were workshop-based and organized by local authorities, voluntary organizations and community groups. Cross (1987a) relates the dichotomous modes of YTS1 to a typology of training which distinguishes the 'vocational' from the 'disciplinary'. For Ainley, however, the ostensible dualism of YTS is something of a facade for the deeper processes of de-skilling and the management of youth, as YTS prepares young people to enter 'an undifferentiated and semi-skilled mass' (1988, p. 83), or keeps them stored for future entry into the workforce. The conceptualization of vocationalism is then problematic, dependent on the extent to which skills are seen as real or bogus and the extent to which YTS has become internally differentiated.

Secondly, as elsewhere, groups who implement public policy also interpret and adapt it. Vocationalism is shaped by administrative and financial structures and by the management practices of those charged to deliver training. Thirdly, within the new vocationalism youth training has been frequently revamped and reformulated since its origins in the mid-1970s. In 1986 YTS was lengthened to a two-year programme of training that combined work experience and off-the-job training. Schemes became more homogeneous and uniform in their treatment of trainees and YTS became uniformly employer-led in philosophy. Like many other administrative changes, this was effected through the financial structuring of schemes. They would now be funded according to their levels of occupancy and on the assumption that wherever possible young people would do their on-the-job training on employers' premises, for which schemes would receive an employers' contribution. This is the phase of YTS which formed the context for research described here: a survey of managing agents conducted in the South West and Liverpool. Within this context there were also regional differences in the prospects for scheme leavers and the structure of youth training. In the South West over 70 per cent of YTS leavers gained jobs, compared with 43 per cent of those in Liverpool. In the South West 8 per cent of training places were premium-funded compared with 36 per cent of places in Liverpool.

Finally, the economic context of training has not been static. YTS emerged in a time of recession and mass youth unemployment but, as Britain moves towards the 1990s, fuller employment, regionalized growth and the expansion of the service sector serve to create a different climate. Youth training appears threatened by fuller employment and new vocationalism seems set for further revision. The paper examines how vocationalism is interpreted and adapted by the scheme managers who deliver it. It raises a number of issues including the changing management structure of schemes and their growing entrepreneurialism, the commodification of young people, their management and control, the perceived relationship between employment, training and qualifications, the nature of employers' present involvement on schemes. It examines what youth training vocationalism becomes in practice and offers a base from which to speculate about the future of YTS as it goes further towards employer-dominated training.

Throughout the paper draws on data collected in a survey of YTS managing agents in Devon, Cornwall and the city of Liverpool between August 1987 and April 1988. Data was collected on 56 managing agencies (27 in the South West and 29 in Liverpool). These managing agencies were all dependent on local employers for work experience placements.

Organizational Change and Management Practice

With the diversity of organizations and the different Modes of YTS it was possible for managing agents to have different approaches and attitudes towards young people. Roberts (1986) has described how firms were using YTS in different ways, to subsidize apprentice training, to screen for employment and as a charitable exercise. Throughout his analysis there is also the theme of cheap labour. Raffe (1986) has categorized schemes in terms of their attachement/detachment to the labour market and their links with educational recruitment. Different training organizations also have different interests, economic and otherwise, in the trainee. Outside company-run schemes, private training agencies (18 per cent of all training places) were formed as businesses, selling training services to the Government and to local employers. This sector of youth training has come in for particular criticism as training for profit has been seen as incompatible with vocationalism (NATFHE, 1984). Voluntary organizations (7 per cent of trainees) and some local authorities (25 per cent of training places) were also involved in training, but these were likely to attract the less able trainee, to train in a workshop form and ally themselves more with youth work. It is amongst these latter schemes the greatest change in YTS2 has been felt. In Liverpool most of the workshop and community-based schemes were run by voluntary and charitable organizations. Here the emphasis was less on employment opportunities and more on life skills, and community service was to the fore. One agent described himself as involved in

> ... not 'real training', apart from training more young people to become aware of social need ... aware of the plight of the handicapped, single parents and the old ... We were not teaching them how to do a job. We're not looking at the theory of wallpaper hanging or anything of that nature.

These changes have had the effect of homogenizing the attitudes of all managing agents who do not control work experience placements themselves; all needed to secure placements with local employers and all needed to obtain employer contributions. Although an additional premium allowance was available for schemes training young people who were relatively unattractive to employers and in places where job prospects were fewer, the allowance covered the cost of retaining trainees in a workshop situation during their first year. It was assumed that by the second year trainees would be placed with an employer. To survive, schemes must be more cost-conscious, and there was increasing and widespread entrepreneurialism among agents, irrespective of the nature of their sponsoring body. With the changes of YTS2 many schemes had become financially independent profit centres in their own right, retaining nominal ties with their sponsoring body and placing greater emphasis on business-based management practice.

Organizational change had altered staff recruitment and usage. This trend was particularly noticeable amongst former workshops. As YOP and YTS1 schemes, they were keen to employ specialist craftsmen, but YTS2 has encouraged schemes to employ managers and administrators, who are needed to deal with the explosion in paperwork that accompanied the change and the marketing of schemes in acquiring and keeping placements. Schemes valued individuals with administrative skills and those familiar with the business world, happy and able to negotiate with and monitor employers. Schemes had expanded with the addition of a second year and this was often seen as requiring tighter control and more support staff.

Linked to these administrative changes, scheme managers widely reported that with YTS2 more emphasis was placed on the qualifications and managerial qualities of staff. These were equated with professionalization. There were a number of indications of this trend: recent recruits were more likely to be graduates; staff development courses were seen as especially important for those with craft backgrounds; one candid manager described how they used to employ 'baby-sitters' under YOP, instructors under YTS1, and with YTS2 they now wanted development and placement officers. The increased professionalism of staff was regarded as another aspect of up-grading youth training and the beginning of a tenuous career structure in YTS management, but it was being achieved at the expense of an existent craft base and artisan employees. As supervisors spent more of their time filling in forms, their craft skills became less important. As managers and administrators were employed, so they knew less about the specific occupational areas involved and scheme officers became more reliant on the knowledge of employers. The new entrant to the staff of YTS schemes had become the manager with a business bias, eager to place young people in the training market and active in the commodification of young people.

There was also a trend towards greater specialization in staff roles within schemes. For example, the manager of an ITEC described how she used to do all the visits and run the scheme; with limited growth but more placements, visiting was now undertaken by a specialist team of four. Schemes' roles had become more clearly defined and the placement officer had emerged as a distinct job. These types of changes could create friction: one scheme was an amalgamation of programmes initially sponsored by Social Services and the local authority, where many longer-standing employees had a youth work approach. With YTS2 the scheme had introduced new management with a more business-orientated managerial style. This had produced a strange mix of staff and some friction as the scheme became more employer-led and attitudes and administrative practices changed.

Managing Young People

A prime issue in a capitalist economy is the control of labour and youth training schemes are central in the management and supervision of young people's labour. When youth unemployment was a more visible issue, new vocationalism identified young people as responsible for their own predicament. They were seen as feckless and unreliable, resistant to the discipline of the workplace and lacking the skills demanded in the present economy or in the future. The emphasis on personal suitability has been further encouraged by the growth of the service sector and the changes in manufacturing processes. All have strengthened management's greater desire for worker control and as managing agents search for work experience placements, pseudo-jobs from employers, they must increasingly bend youth training to suit employer-demand.

In the survey all scheme managers sought discipline, punctuality, reliability and obedience from their trainees. For some this was central to their training objectives and for others it was more peripheral or unstated. Life skill elements were central to the courses offered by premium schemes but additional to mainly basic schemes which concentrated on specialized and specific vocational courses. Another version of life skills was found in the basic schemes that taught 'enterprise skills'. Although it was recognized that few trainees would move from YTS into self-employment, these courses imbued young people with an individualized approach to work and implanted the ambition of self-employment firmly in their minds as a future option.

Management interests have merged with those of other agencies and YTS can be included within a more coherent state-directed youth policy (Davies, 1986). The young unemployed have few options other than to join a scheme, especially since the withdrawal of income support from those under 18. In the past unqualified school-leavers were an unstable part of the labour market, dipping in and out of employment with short spells on the dole. For Hamilton (1987) the main objective of a youth programme is to end this period of floundering, to smooth and organize the passage to employment. These changes form part of the wider bureaucratization of youth and youth issues (see Wallace, forthcoming).

As the training schemes surveyed filtered young people into jobs, selectivity was a constant. The better the job prospects of scheme leavers the more likely schemes were to be selective about entrants. Some administered tests, others screened for severe disability, behavioural problems and criminal records and yet more admitted trainees only once an employer had agreed to provide them with a work experience placement. More selectivity and screening occurred once trainees were in schemes. It was normal practice for agencies that specialized in premium trainees to screen carefully before they were sent out to placement; new employers would 'get the best' and employers who had been disappointed with earlier trainees were given 'better' ones next time; placements were organized so that they took it in turns to have 'good and bad lads'. It was widely seen as a better organizational practice to keep trainees within schemes than to send them out ill-prepared and ill-suited to employer demands. 'It's no use sending them out if the next day they are back'. Unsatisfied employers would then be likely to look to other managing agents to supply more reliable trainees or not use YTS at all.

As training agencies without internal placements were encouraged to become more entrepreneurial, obtaining contributions became a major preoccupation. Set charges and fixed scales dominated the pricing of basic trainees and managing agents commonly obtained between £13 and £15 for these trainees from employers. The picture for premium schemes was rather different. They had fewer trainees out on placement, a lower level of employer contribution and more 'free places'. They were also the schemes where employers were most likely to default on their agreed contributions. If contributions for premium trainees was obtained at all, most were of the order of £5 to £10 and the rates were always negotiable. Although all trainees appeared to be being bought and sold in the training market, some agents in charitable organizations were regretful about these developments. They disliked the implications of selling trainees and the price element in poaching placements and undercutting other agents. 'To say "You can have them for £10 or, if you take two disabled, you can have them for a fiver each" — that's a frightening thing. The trainee is just being treated as a commodity.'

In placing trainees with work experience providers, most agencies adopted the model of the employment agency. They suited employers' needs by sending a number of trainees to interviews and letting the employer then choose. A number linked this practice to a training rationale; it simulated a real job application; it taught them about interviews; it was better for them to learn to be refused on a training scheme than learn these bitter lessons when making real job applictions. A number of agencies claimed that increasingly employers were coming to agencies already with a selected trainee and the agent was asked to organize YTS for the pair.

Many agents reported that most placements were lost by trainees because of absence or bad time-keeping rather than bad workmanship. Here pre-placement screening ensured that trainees would be sent out only when the agent was sure that they would turn up regularly for work. Alternatively clashes of personality were seen as responsible for friction and dissatisfaction in placements. Throughout it was never thought to be the job. As all efforts were in the direction of sifting and matching, with financial penalties for agents with high rates of moving or large proportions of trainees drifting between schemes, the early training behaviour of young people today may be considerably more stable than their employment behaviour in an earlier era.

The other major way in which agents lost placements was through trainees being offered employment by the placement provider or finding a job elsewhere. If this occurred at the end of training it was largely welcomed by the agents — even though employment might remove the place from use by subsequent trainees — as it boosted the credibility of their scheme. Another element which affected placements was the negotiations which went on with employers about the level of training which trainees would be expected to engage in. In some placements where there is a chance of a job, 'the emphasis there is on halting progress in his training programme and concentrating on what that employer wants, which means we won't end up with the appropriate piece of paper that we first thought essential.' Here the retention of the placement and the prospect of a job were seen as not entirely compatible with training, but such trade-offs, where vocationalism appears at odds with employment, contain a gamble for the trainee.

Whatever the training objectives of YTS, there was a widespread reluctance to move trainees between placements and job-tasting was rare. Universally it was argued that moving trainees might enhance vocational knowledge and experience but it undermined job prospects. This was especially so if the trainee was receiving valued training, since their movement between employers opened up the possibility of poaching by another firm. Hence they were only moved where agents had established that there was no chance of employment, but even here there were pressures against this happening. Systematic movement was too difficult logistically and it upset employers to lose the services of trainees, even those whom they had no intention of employing.

The interstitial position of managing agents made their relations with employers complex. Although managing agents monitored employers for gross infringement of training rules, they also interpreted and defended them against public policy and attempted to win their cooperation in providing the placements upon which their agency depended. One agent described his role as to 'teach employers to use MSC jargon', so that they could parcel unaltered ways of behaving towards young people in the new wrapping of contemporary youth training policy. Many toned down their monitoring visits so that they would not appear intrusive and over-demanding.

> You have to have a balance. Some of these placement providers are very busy people. That's an area where we tread lightly. We get the information we require but we can't go in with a full list of competence objectives to do a progress report . . . The provider would not put up with that, but he would let a supervisor chat about things while you are making notes. You try to impose paperwork and get them to write anything down, then you are asking for complaints.

In a poor employment situation and where placement providers were small firms, agents were forced to be minimalist in their approach. Monitoring visits were also a form of surreptitious marketing for agents. They checked that providers were content, attempted to nip any problems with trainees in the bud, and looked for further training places. Also some agents described attempts to involve employers more in training as a losing battle, since it was often hard to get employers involved in the Programme Review Teams. Scheme managers largely regarded themselves as operating amid employers' widespread indifference to training and such responses seem unlikely to change as schemes become employer-owned.

Labour and Training

The development of an employer-led YTS has raised issues about the relationship between labour, production and its reward. With the introduction of employer-led YTS the differences between training and producing became blurred. As YTS moves to become employer-owned and off-the-job training becomes more flexible, the differences will be further eroded. To date the debates in this area have been concerned with the cheapening of youth labour and the replacement of jobs by training places. There is however another issue in that managing agents who are not employers may use trainees in selling scheme services and manufacturing products. Almost half the schemes surveyed derived some income from the sale of the scheme's products and services. Many of the agents described their involvements as 'not serious', as 'only bits and pieces' or claimed they were reliant on a word-of-mouth clientele. Schemes were variously involved in the sale of computer components, small electrical or motor repairs, the manufacture of soft toys, garden furniture and printed mirrors, re-upholstery and dress alterations, and it was premium trainees who were most involved in this fringe production. Although many agents currently saw these developments as generating windfall profits, others claimed to be increasingly thinking in this entrepreneurial direction. They were thinking more in the way of the small firm, a curious twist on the theme of becoming more employer-led. It was also another way in which youth training was sliding more obviously into youth workfare.

Although a number of agents were interested in boosting production, all acknowledged that this developmental path contained difficulties and pitfalls. A frequent comment was that productive enterprise was incompatible with training and its introduction or extension would subvert the aims of the organization and create a conflict of interest. One horticultural scheme was contemplating selling more of its produce and modifying what it grew to this end, and this envisaged compromise of training and production was a field devoted to cut flowers and smaller experimental allotments kept for purely training purposes. However, as vocationalism merged with work, contradictions emerged for independent training agencies. A regime of 'real work' could be inimical to their relationship with trainees:

> [Doing furniture repairs] is fine if your trainees are fit and able and can cope, but if they are not able and Mrs Smith wants her wardrobe or her bed and the trainee has got a problem, we can stop. You can't if you are producing for someone else.

Scheme personnel became more involved in work supervision and quality control. Product liability became a problem and 'real work' could also diminish any training content.

> In the real world of work, say for instance in sewing, all you are doing is putting a sleeve in, putting a neck band on or putting an arm in, which gets very repetitive and boring for the youngsters.

Here accurate simulations of the work environment appeared to diminish the quality of training and were often described as a distraction from the main tasks of agents; such experiences of 'real work' were only valid as part of a 'real job'. Most agents concentrated their efforts on finding employer placements and securing employer contributions as these were more valuable as a training experience, in profit terms and for future job prospects.

Community based schemes had changed most with the adoption of a more entrepreneurial approach. They had historically been involved in tasks in the community for which only a small or no charge was made. They did jobs referred to them by social services or local charities and gave preference to those least able to pay commercial rates. The community approach used the unpaid labour of trainees for charitable ends and as this approach has become progressively harder to integrate within YTS, schemes were considering offering these services on a new commercial basis.

Training and Qualifications

New vocationalism has sought to restructure and improve vocational qualifications. New vocational qualifications became available, and established ones systematized, with the work of the National Council for Vocational Qualification (NCVQ). Despite this there is no national accreditation of YTS in England and vocationalism had conserved existing divisions in patterns of occupational recruitment, relative to school streaming, ethnicity and gender.

New vocationalism has ushered in a new vocabulary for training programmes and qualifications, with skills-testing, competence objectives and profiling. The survey looked at how managing agents approached these qualifications.

The schemes were offering a huge array of courses and qualifications, but as in a national profile, these were dominated by City and Guilds and RSA courses. However, although vocational qualifications have a higher profile in YTS2, out of the fifty-five managing agencies surveyed, six stated that they were not offering vocational qualifications to all their trainees. Also a number of the remainder admitted that although vocational qualifications were on offer to all trainees, not everyone was taking them. They identified a number of reasons for this. Firstly, some trainees were described as uninterested in courses that smacked of school. Secondly, there was the lack of suitable courses. A third reason was the cost of bought-in courses. Some agents wanted evidence of aptitude prior to sponsoring trainees to do courses and others were asking employers to contribute additionally for examination fees. As cash limits for schemes and the courses trainees pursued were stringently and uniformly applied, examination entry was no longer unlimited.

In addition, managing agents were asked if they had any difficulty in finding a suitable vocational course and qualification for their trainees; 42 per cent (twenty-three schemes) claimed that they did. When pressed the areas of difficulty were two-fold. Nine agents had difficulty gaining access to the right type of course for trainees in particular training areas and this seemed a particular problem for those in hand craft skills. Another area of difficulty, raised by thirteen schemes, was the level at which vocational qualifications started, relative to the abilities of trainees presently on schemes. They felt that all courses presupposed basic numeracy and literacy and contained theoretical elements which were beyond the reach of the really low achiever. It was felt that vocational courses could not compensate for deficiencies in Maths and English, areas vital to vocational success. Schemes aimed at the low achiever preferred to concentrate on basic numeracy and literacy and life skills rather than attempt further qualifications. They often used their own assessment system, where any change in the response of trainees was marked as an improvement. Here assessment was a means of boosting self-confidence and eliciting cooperation and it was geared to enable all to pass. For these types of schemes NCVQ was a distant, ivory-tower movement, insensitive to the consequences of its policies on 'an organization like ours, a charity-based, low-achiever organization'.

Some managing agents talked in terms of finer gradations of trainees, and drew a distinction between 'premiums' and 'super-premiums'. These thought that not all trainees would obtain vocational qualifications. This is supported by the national profile of qualifications gained by YTS trainees in their first year; while the national entry for qualifications approached 100 per cent in all types of agency, over 60 per cent of ITEC trainees had gained a qualification during their first year, compared with between 50 per cent and 60 per cent of trainees in private and public sector schemes and less than 40 per cent of those in schemes sponsored by voluntary associations. The survey also suggested that the recorded high level of entry may be something of a fiction: not all those following a course may be entered for an examination; some agents noted that non-attendance at courses sub-contracted out to colleges was not uncommon and that there was little that could be done about this. Another admitted that it was their policy to turn a blind eye to such non-attendance as this was often the least popular part of the training and they did not want the trainee to abandon the scheme altogether if reprimanded on this issue.

Managing agents of YTS are required to provide trainees with a minimum of twenty weeks off-the-job training throughout their two years on a scheme. Traditionally, vocational training for skilled manual and routine white collar work had been the preserve of the further education college. However, the survey suggested that increasingly its facilities are not being used by YTS schemes. The modularization of courses and the specification of subject areas and core skills has enabled managing agents to piece together a short-course training structure and to undertake more of the training themselves. In the funding structure of YTS2 there were cost-savings to be made by training in-house.

Of those surveyed, fifteen schemes were providing all the off-the-job training themselves, thirty-seven schemes were providing off-the-job training using a mix of themselves, colleges and other training agencies and two schemes had sub-contracted all off-the-job training to a further education college. College courses, often viewed as expensive and inflexible by managing agents, were characteristically used for specific vocational teaching, whereas personal effectiveness and communication skills were taught in-house and computer literacy, if not taught by the agent themselves, was purchased from a college or another agency. Managing agencies also exchanged training, a move which entirely by-passed colleges. All suggested the new competitive edge there was in this educational sector and the fluidity of the changes.

Vocationalism was interpreted in different ways by different schemes. The renewed emphasis on vocational qualifications fitted in more easily with the existent practices of basic schemes training for a particularly skilled niche in the labour market. Some schemes reported a recent move towards streaming their trainees to maximize the qualifications attained. The emphasis on relevant courses also moved thinking away from notions of portable skills towards training for specific tasks and towards the current work experience place or job in hand. Concepts of general vocationalism and multi-skilling were then subverted by commitment to an employer-led philosophy, but some job prospects could be enhanced by less contact with employers. One ITEC manager described how that scheme had reorganized training to promote a more concentrated learning within particular specialisms, spent less time with employers and undertook more off-the-job training. He claimed that subsequently trainees had performed better in their examinations and secured better jobs. Where the attachment was not to a real but a notional employer, commitment to transferable skills still dominated. Furthermore, the increased emphasis on training for vocational qualifications was encouraging voluntary organizations to supplant task force activities in the community with in-house instruction, although training became less 'real' or relevant to the locality.

A programme of vocational preparation is also problematic when many did not enter jobs for which they were ostensibly being trained. Not all could mimic the training programmes of elite schemes, central to company recruitment, and some managers in premium schemes expressed concern about the over-certification of trainees, where 'you seem to be getting City and Guilds qualifications in being able to clock in and out'. In the certification of vocationalism, managers had to elicit the cooperation of employers. Work-based progress sheets were central to the process but on the whole managing agents seemed concerned not to over-tax employers with paper-work. Sheets were filled in either by the trainees or during monitoring by the scheme representative and then initialled by the supervisor.

Skills testing has become more formally built into the system of assessment and certification and in this more was demanded of employers. Here Caterbase is an example: employers with trainees following Caterbase courses, with its skills-tested modules, are required to complete a short training course themselves. They are then seen as equipped to assess the proficiency of their trainee in the different elements of catering and award the relevant certificate. Some agents were apprehensive about such a system. They felt that only the larger and more up-market employers would commit themselves and their time to participating in the training days. Trainees at the bottom end of the market would then not be eligible for these qualifications. Also there was some doubt about the capacity of smaller employers to judge the work of trainees and doubt about the comparability of standards across the industry. The skills certificate would then only be as good as the skills of the employer who examines it and the placement where it is gained. In British youth training there is no attempt to control the quality of employers as trainers as does the '*Meister*' system of Germany where craftsmen are judged and licensed to pass their skills on to a trainee.

Vocationalism weakened as trainees were in situations more marginal to the labour market and agents recognized the gap between training titles, what trainees were doing and where they would be subsequently employed; 'I tell the trainees that although they spend a lot of their time painting and decorating, they are really construction workers, but they know that really the work and the money is in hod-carrying and general labouring.'

Some schemes retained a more obvious welfare stance but felt that in the contemporary interpretation of vocationalism this was under-valued and ignored. They thought there was too little appreciation of the range of young people that entered YTS or the amount of time that 'problem youngsters' could take.

> The MSC contacted me and said 'Have you got any success stories?' and I said, 'Well, we've got one that you could print, we've taken two trainees off drugs and stopped another from stealing.' But they are not really interested and these are things they can't print. This isn't what they think of as success.

The interpretation of vocationalism varied with the scheme's position within the local labour and training market. Vocational qualifications also reflected short-term interests as they were subsumed within the greater efforts of agencies to please employers and were relevant only so far as they enhanced worker virtues or suited the immediate wants of employers.

Conclusion

Unemployment is no longer the topical issue it once was. Reported increases in job vacancies and the policy changes for the unemployed have shortened the recorded length of the dole queue. Unemployment has also receded from the public imagination as people and the media now concentrate their anxiety on the environment and the health service. As unemployment retreats in popular thinking so the issues of new vocationalism recede in importance. In the past new vocationalism in the shape of YTS has been subject to constant change and revision. This paper has discussed its relationship to YTS managing agents and how they interpreted and implemented an employer-led programme of vocational training.

Employer-led YTS has had a number of consequences for schemes. This development is an example of privatization as a management practice. Here the Government continues to supply and control the bulk of training funds, but to devolve responsibility to private and public agencies, which in turn have become more entrepreneurial in their approach to employers and in their use of staff and trainees. The Government retains central and ultimate control through its financial structures but sheds responsibility. The changes are not unique to youth training as the managing agency is a structure which is beginning to dominate in the privatization of welfare, individualizing issues and promoting entrepreneurialism.

Managing agents have become more entrepreneurial in their relationships with trainees. Staff are required to be more proficient in management and marketing and young people are more carefully screened and, where their acceptability to employers is in doubt, more closely monitored. As schemes compete for the favours of local employers they may engage in the struggle for placements and employer contributions and negotiate the content and extent of training more closely with employers. An employer-led YTS has more thoroughly commodified young people and their labour. These trends will be extended in the envisaged hand-over of YTS control to local groups of employers in the proposed Technical and Enterprise Councils.

The relationship between vocationalism and employer-ledness is particularly relevant today as YTS is poised on the brink of new developments. The White Paper, *Employment in the 1990s*, has invited groups of local employers to submit proposals for the establishment of Training and Enterprise Councils in their district. These TECs will be repsonsible for the development of training and the promotion of small businesses within their area. The Training Agency (erstwhile the MSC) seems set to withdraw from training, to end its more radical intervention in youth training programmes. Although the Government will continue for the time being to finance the bulk of training, it hopes 'to place ''ownership'' of the training and enterprise system where it belongs — with employers' (HMSO, 1988, p. 40). Later it is anticipated that the financial rug will be pulled from beneath the schemes and employers also expected progressively to fund training themselves. With unemployment out of the headlines, the Government is retreating from the centrally directed imposition of a training culture and re-delivering training once more into the hands of local employers. As Britain moves towards an 'employer-owned' YTS the trend extends elements established in the employer-led system.

The future of YTS is uncertain. As Ainley commented, 'Nobody doubts that, in the extremely unlikely event of the much promised upturn returning the economy to full employment, YTS would be quietly forgotten' (1988, p. 113). But if it does not disappear YTS seems set to become more differentiated locally. It will reinforce the tendency for regional decentralization and the devolution of training to more local units. This will extend present trends as YTS in the more prosperous South East can concentrate on specific skills training for trainees, many of whom have employed status. It may continue to be used as a palliative to the lingering unemployment of the depressed regions, but this is more problematic. Employer-owned training presupposes a depth of training knowledge, interest and expertise amongst employers, little of which were evident in the research.

Chapter 7

A Decade of Decline:
Social Class and Post-school Destinations of Minimum-age School-leavers in Scotland, 1977–1987

Andy Furlong

Introduction

The period since 1977 has been characterized by a 'new vocationalism' involving the development and proliferation of training schemes and courses. Whilst these developments should have resulted in new opportunities which might in turn have reduced class inequalities there has been a marked absence of research addressing these questions. Despite the vast changes in the nature of the transition from school, most of our knowledge of the differential effects of unemployment is at the level of educational attainment groups. Our knowledge of the effects of the changes in terms of social class has tended to come from small scale studies or else is inferred from the known links between educational outcomes and social class.

In the 1960s and early 1970s, in many parts of Britain, young people often made a more or less direct transition from school to work, perhaps broken by a short spell of unemployment. This was particularly true for those young people, often from working-class families, who had low educational qualifications (Ashton and Field, 1976). Those with higher qualifications often made their transition via an extended period of post-16 education or training. In some cases this took the form of a short vocational course at a college of further education, while for others it took the form of a longer transition pattern via a period of post-compulsory schooling and often higher education before starting work. During the 1970s levels of school-leaver unemployment rose and the proportion of young people entering full-time employment on leaving school steadily declined. This trend became particularly severe after 1979 (Raffe, 1983a).

The decline of the youth labour market has had far-reaching effects on the transition from school which have been subject to detailed examination in recent sociological work (for example: Raffe, 1984a, 1988a; Ashton *et al.*, 1982; Brown and Ashton, 1987; Furlong, 1987a, 1987b). Through this literature we already know much about the effects of economic and institutional change on young people. We know that the loss of youth jobs and the experience of unemployment have disproportionately affected unqualified young people (Ashton *et al.*, 1982; Raffe, 1983b), and that the decline in job opportunities has been associated with a rise in the proportion of young people, especially females, who enter post-compulsory education (Raffe, 1984b; Furlong, 1986). We also know that work experience schemes such as the Job Creation Programme (JCP) and the Youth Opportunities Programme (YOP) mainly recruited unqualified young people (Raffe, 1984c). Recently there have been attempts to attract more qualified school-leavers on to schemes with the introduction of the Youth Training Scheme (YTS), yet the composition of schemes is still skewed towards lower qualified young people (Raffe, 1988c).

The aim of this paper is to examine some of the effects of the decline in the youth labour market over the decade 1977 to 1987, for young people who left school at the minimum age, in terms of class, in order to see whether class inequalities have been reduced. I will do this by using data from the Scottish School Leavers Surveys. First I describe the changes in school-leaver destinations in general terms and put this into a social class perspective in order to show the differences in transitional patterns among young people from different social classes and to highlight any changes which may have occurred over the decade. Secondly, I look at the relative chances of young people from different social classes with different qualifications entering a 'reasonable job' after leaving school. Thirdly, I examine the relative chances of young people from different social classes and with different qualifications of avoiding 'long-term' unemployment in the immediate post-school period.

Data and Methods

The Scottish School Leavers Surveys are postal surveys which have been carried out at Edinburgh University by the Centre for Educational Sociology since 1971. Since 1977, the surveys have been undertaken every two years. School-leavers are selected by birthdate from a sampling frame which includes all Scottish schools except special schools. The sampling fraction of the data set used here consists of 10 per cent of Scottish school-leavers in the years 1979, 1981, 1983, 1985 and 1987. The 1977 data set contains 10 per cent of school-leavers in four selected regions.

The data which were used for the year 1977 are confined to four areas: Strathclyde, Lothian, Fife and Tayside. This is because data collected in the other regions in 1977 was confined to qualified school-leavers. However, about three-quarters of the population of Scotland reside in these four regions. In this paper only these four areas are used in analysis of factors relating to 1977. Data for the other years were collected from a representative national sample. In relation to long-term unemployment it has been necessary to look at trends from 1979 onwards as from the 1977 questionnaires it was not always possible to determine whether a young person had spent a part of their time since leaving school on a work experience scheme.

The questionnaires were sent out in the spring, about ten months after the majority of young people had left school. Thus the 1977 survey covers those who had left school during the academic year 1975/76, while the 1987 survey covered 1985/86 leavers. Typical response rates were in the region of 80 per cent (details of the sample and response rates have been described in Raffe, 1988a). As a result of the information collected in these surveys, we are able to report on the changes affecting school-leavers in Scotland over a decade which has seen a radical restructuring of the youth labour market. There is no comparable data source for England which covers this period with a national sample, but information from the Scottish surveys can help in the understanding of changes in the English labour market insofar as it is 'not wholly misleading to treat Scotland as a 'microcosm' of Great Britain' (Raffe and Courtenay, 1988).

Although the Scottish School Leavers Surveys covered leavers from fourth, fifth and sixth years, the analysis in this paper is confined to minimum-age school-leavers. Minimum-age school-leavers are defined as those who had left school by the end of the fourth year (16-year-olds), but also include some young people who, because of their birthdates, were unable to leave until Christmas of the fifth year and left at that stage. (Young people start their secondary education a year later in Scotland than in England and so the Scottish fourth year is broadly equivalent to the English fifth year.) In Scotland the leaving pattern is more complex than in England, and nearly 30 per cent of the year group are too young to leave at the end of the fourth year. This group, often referred to as the 'conscripts', have to stay at school until the Christmas of the fifth year. As a result of changes affecting primary school entrance, the proportion of young people having to stay on into the fifth year has increased in recent years (Burnhill, 1984).

Class analysis is based upon the Registrar General's social classes using the young people's fathers' current or most recent occupation. Although this is the classification used in official statistics and much Government sponsored work, in many respects the Registrar General's social classes are unsatisfactory (Bland, 1979). In addition, use of the male occupation can obscure important differences within families and I would agree that cross-class analysis provides definite advantages. This paper is based on fathers' occupations mainly because mothers' occupations were not collected in 1979 and 1981. Even then, because details of mothers' current or last occupation were collected it may distort women's class position. Women's status in the labour market tends to change considerably through their life-cycle (Hakim, 1979; Martin and Roberts, 1984) and status of mothers with teenage children may not accurately represent their true skill levels. A more accurate picture of women's social class may be gathered through questions which ask for 'best' occupation or for details of occupations they were trained in. Yet in a postal questionnaire which collects details of parental occupation through young people this would probably be too complex and might be misleading.

The data for each year were weighted to compensate for differential non-response, so that the weighted distribution of sample members matched figures provided by the Scottish Education Department for sex and total Scottish Certificate of Education attainment.

The Changes

Turning now to examine the changes in the destinations of minimum-age school-leavers over the decade 1977 to 1987 (Table 7.1), it is clear that the most notable change has been the steep decline in the proportion of leavers who entered full-time employment. In the spring of 1977, 72 per cent of 1976 minimum-age school-leavers were in full-time employment. In contrast, in the spring of 1987, only 26 per cent of 1986 school-leavers were in full-time employment. In 1977 it was very common for minimum-age school-leavers to be in a full-time job by the spring after leaving school, in 1987 it was relatively rare.

Table 7.1: Spring destinations of minimum-age school-leavers: 1977 to 1987 (%)

	1977*	1979	1981	1983	1985	1987
Schemes	5	8	18	25	30	43
Full-time job	72	72	57	42	37	26
Unemployed	16	12	18	21	22	20·*
Full-time education	5	6	6	8	6	7
Other	3	2	1	4	4	3
Unweighted n	(2302)	(3756)	(3113)	(3690)	(3110)	(2110)
Total	101	100	100	100	99	99

Notes:
* 1977 figures are based on four regions (Strathclyde, Lothian, Fife and Tayside).
  Destinations are self-reported, unemployment is defined as 'unemployed and looking for work'.

Over this same period the unemployment rate among minimum-age leavers in the spring after leaving school rose from 16 per cent in 1977 to a peak of 22 per cent in 1985. Yet the collapse in the youth labour market was not wholly reflected in the unemployment figures. The discrepancy between the sharp fall in jobs and the not so steep rise in unemployment was mainly accounted for by the growth of work experience and training schemes for young people (from 5 per cent of minimum-age leavers in 1977 to 43 per cent in 1987) as well as an increase in participation in post-compulsory education.

Partly as a consequence of the decline in job opportunities for school-leavers, more young people now stay on at school after it ceases to be compulsory (Raffe, 1984b). In 1977 the majority of young people in Scotland had left school by end of their fourth year (59 per cent), yet by 1987 the proportion leaving by the end of the fourth year had fallen by 18 percentage points to 41 per cent. Further, throughout the decade, there was a growth in the proportion of young people who entered some form of education after leaving school, although entrants to non-advanced further education tend to complete their fifth year at school (Furlong and Raffe, 1989).

Table 7.2: Spring destinations of minimum-age school-leavers, by social class: 1977 to 1987 (%)

	Schemes	Job	Unemployed	Education	Other	Unweighted n	Total	% leaving school at minimum age	Unweighted n (base)
Class I & II									
1977*	1	77	10	10	2	(237)	100	34	(843)
1979	5	76	6	12	1	(420)	100	35	(1377)
1981	7	73	9	10	1	(339)	100	27	(1383)
1983	17	51	13	16	4	(386)	101	26	(1632)
1985	25	51	12	9	2	(347)	99	25	(1535)
1987	39	31	16	11	2	(294)	99	22	(1557)
% change 1977–1987	+38	−46	+6	+1	0			−12	
Class IIIn & IIIm									
1977*	5	75	13	4	2	(1180)	99	71	(1884)
1979	8	76	10	5	1	(1714)	100	72	(2499)
1981	19	58	16	6	1	(1497)	100	68	(2390)
1983	25	44	19	8	3	(1832)	99	59	(3174)
1985	32	39	20	6	3	(1266)	100	57	(2442)
1987	46	28	16	7	3	(916)	100	44	(2230)
% change 1977–1987	+41	−47	+3	+3	+1			−27	
Class IV & V									
1977*	5	70	19	3	2	(520)	99	77	(740)
1979	6	72	14	5	1	(855)	98	82	(1073)
1981	20	52	20	7	1	(728)	100	78	(998)
1983	27	42	20	6	5	(764)	100	70	(1118)
1985	28	40	22	6	4	(597)	100	65	(990)
1987	47	24	20	5	4	(369)	100	48	(822)
% change 1977–1987	+42	−46	+1	+2	+2			−29	

Notes:
* 1977 figures are based on four regions (Strathclyde, Lothian, Fife and Tayside).
Destinations are self reported, unemployment is defined as 'unemployed and looking for work'.

When these changes are looked at in terms of social class (Table 7.2), we can see that the decline has affected young people in different ways. First, in 1977 young people from classes I & II and IIIn & IIIm were more likely to be in jobs in the spring after leaving than were young people from classes IV & V. The same was true in 1987. Similarly, in 1977 and 1987 those from classes I & II were less likely to be unemployed than those from classes IV & V, and also less likely to be on a work experience or training scheme.

The inequalities which exist between the classes are not new, yet in terms of minimum-age school-leavers, the inequalities seem not to have widened during the recession. The percentage fall in the proportion of young people who were in full-time jobs in the spring between 1977 and 1987 was similar for all classes; 46 points for class I and II, 47 points for those from class IIIn and IIIm and 46 points for class IV & V. The rise in spring unemployment was greater among school-leavers from class I & II at 6 percentage points than among those from classes IIIn and IIIm and IV & V.

The increase in unemployment over this period was not a linear trend. It tended to fall between 1977 and 1979, and increase again between 1979 and 1981 (Raffe, 1984b). Making a straightforward comparison between 1977 and 1987 is misleading as the increase in unemployment occurs earlier for young people from class IIIn & IIIm and class IV & V than for those from class I & II. If we look at the percentage rise in unemployment between the highest and lowest points within each social class, the rise is more equitable. Unemployment among those from class I & II rose by 10 percentage points (between 1979 and 1987), class IIIn & IIIm by 10 precentage points (between 1979 and 1985) and class IV & V by 8 percentage points (between 1979 and 1985). Between 1985 and 1987 there was a fall in unemployment for class IIIn & IIIm and class IV & V, but this did not affect young people with fathers in class I & II.

Since their inception, the social composition of schemes has been skewed towards young people with lower qualification levels and those with fathers employed in manual occupations (Raffe, 1984c; Seale, 1985). Although the current scheme, YTS, was intended to have a broader appeal, in Chapter 4 of this volume Raffe argues that YTS has had little effect on well qualified school-leavers. When we look at scheme participation in terms of social class, we see that the level of participation among young people from class I & II was always lower than among young people from other classes. There was also a different pattern in uptake. The increase in the proportion of young people on schemes in the spring between 1977 and 1987 was 38 percentage points for those from class I & II, 41 percentage points for those from class IIIn & IIIm and 42 percentage points for those from class IV & V.

Young people from class I & II also tended to be slower in taking up places on schemes. For those with fathers in class IIIn & IIIm and class IV & V there were big increases in the proportion on schemes between 1979 and 1981 and again between 1983 and 1985 and 1985 and 1987. For those from class I & II the first main increase came later, between 1981 and 1983 and then increased relatively slowly until between 1985 and 1987 when participation increased at a similar rate to those from the other classes.

As the level of unemployment rose and as schemes increasingly became a first post-school destination for minimum-age leavers, more young people decided to stay on at school beyond the minimum age. This was true within each class, although the proportional decrease in minimum-age school-leavers was greater within class IV & V and IIIn & IIIm than within class I & II.

Social Class, Qualifications and 'Reasonable Jobs'

In the previous section I have discussed some of the class variation in the post-school destinations of minimum-age school-leavers. In this section, I concentrate on the types of jobs young people entered. Among young people who were working in the spring after leaving, there were marked differences in the types of work they were doing. These differences may be partly explained by social class.

I have already remarked that job entry by the spring after leaving school became less common as the decade progressed and schemes became established routes into the labour market. Because of schemes, the transition from school to work has become more protracted and it is less satisfactory to comment on young people's transitions at a point ten months after the majority left school. Due to the normality of schemes as part of the transition by the mid-eighties, the only available occupational outcome for many young people is that of YTS placement occupation. To the extent that YTS occupation is often conditional and subject to confirmation or change on leaving the scheme, this is an unsatisfactory occupational measure. Nevertheless, longitudinal work on young people in Scotland has demonstrated that, generally, there was a high level of continuity between YTS placements and subsequent employment

(Furlong and Raffe, 1989) — although the relationship between YOP placements and subsequent employment may have been different.

The first job a young person enters has an important effect on subsequent employment (Payne, 1987), and we are able to use details of first occupation as an indicator of future life chances. Although there were some occupations in which there was a lower probability of post-scheme retention (such as shopwork) the outflows from schemes rarely crossed broad occupational divisions. At this stage in the transiton there is little point in using a detailed job classification or in trying to predict future class positions.

Although there have been attempts to develop youth class categories (Jones, 1987) which can be useful in studies of mobility among young people, these have been identified longitudinally and are based on a combination of social class of origin and young people's occupations at the age of 23. The young people covered by the Scottish School Leavers Surveys had only been out of school for an average of ten months. As many young people came to enter work experience and training schemes, it became more common for young people to have had experience of more than one occupation in the period after leaving school (although movement tended to be within a broad occupational band). A detailed occupational classification used in conjunction with other variables would produce small cell sizes and make the predictions less reliable. Here I dichotomize job types into 'reasonable jobs' and 'bad jobs'.

In the 'bad jobs' category I have included semi- and unskilled manual work and routine shop work. This sort of work rarely provides opportunities for advancement and has been described as 'careerless' work (Ashton and Field, 1976). The 'reasonable jobs' category basically includes all other jobs, that is, managerial, professional and related, technical, clerical and skilled manual. Jobs in this category usually provide some opportunities for career advancement; it combines jobs categorized by Ashton and Field (1976) as 'working-class career jobs' and 'long-term career jobs' (relatively few minimum-age leavers entered 'long-term career jobs').

In Table 7.3 we can see the proportion of minimum-age school-leavers who entered 'reasonable jobs' from each social class between 1977 and 1987. The proportion entering these jobs declined from 1979 through to 1985, although there was an increase in the proportion of young people from class IV & V who entered 'reasonable jobs' between 1985 and 1987.

In each year there was a strong class differential in the proportion obtaining 'reasonable jobs'. There was always a greater proportion of young

Table 7.3: Minimum-age leavers who entered a 'reasonable' job by spring, by social class; 1977 to 1987 (%)

	1977*	1979	1981	1983	1985	1987
Class I & II	81	81	74	68	70	69
Class IIIn & IIIm	74	74	68	65	63	62
Class IV & V	63	66	54	54	54	59
Difference between Class I & II and Class IIIn & IIIm	−7	−7	−6	−3	−7	−7
Difference between Class IIIn & IIIm and Class IV & V	−11	−8	−14	−11	−9	−3
Difference between Class I & II and Class IV & V	−18	−15	−20	−14	−16	−10
Unweighted n(base)	(2152)	(3205)	(2365)	(2629)	(1828)	(2556)

Notes:
* 1977 figures are based on four regions (Strathclyde, Lothian, Fife and Tayside).

people with fathers in class I & II who entered 'reasonable jobs', followed by class IIIn & IIIm, with those from class IV & V consistently obtaining the lowest proportion. The difference between class IV & V and class I & II fluctuated between years, but the net change, either across the decade or between 1979 and 1987, did not result in wider class differentials. Between 1977 and 1987, the difference between class IV & V and class I & II narrowed by 8 points (from a difference of 18 percentage points to 10 percentage points), while if we take the years 1979 to 1987 the differential narrowed by 5 percentage points (from 15 percentage points to 10 percentage points).

The influence of social class of origin on the likelihood of entering certain types of job is largely mediated through educational qualifications (Heath, 1981). Any changes in the occupational distributions of school-leavers from different social classes may be partly a result of a change in relative educational successes, and there is evidence to suggest that the change to comprehensive schooling in Scotland has benefited young people from working-class families in terms of qualifications (McPherson and Willms, 1987). This could explain the narrowing of class differentials in the proportion entering 'reasonable jobs'.

In order to assess the relative influence of social class and qualifications, I constructed a Logit model (separately for males and females) to predict the relative chances of certain 'types' of minimum-age school-leaver having entered a 'reasonable job' by the spring after school leaving (Table 7.4). In this

Table 7.4: Logit model predicting relative chances of minimum-age school-leavers having entered a 'reasonable' job (compared to social class I & II with five or more O grades in 1977)

	Male			Female		
	Relative chances	GLIM coefficient	(se)	Relative chances	GLIM coefficient	(se)
Class IIIn & IIIm	1.3	0.2663	(0.08)	0.7	−0.3146	(0.10)
Class IV & V	0.9	−0.1170	(0.09)	0.6	−0.5519	(0.11)
3–4 O grades	0.8	−0.1924	(0.15)	0.9	−0.1449	(0.17)
1–2 O grades	0.5	−0.6756	(0.13)	0.4	−1.037	(0.16)
No award/DE	0.2	−1.438	(0.12)	0.2	−1.678	(0.15)
1979	0.9	−0.06473	(0.09)	0.9	−0.1015	(0.10)
1981	0.7	−0.3565	(0.10)	0.5	−0.7353	(0.11)
1983	0.8	−0.2424	(0.10)	0.4	−0.9874	(0.12)
1985	0.6	−0.4535	(0.12)	0.3	−1.099	(0.13)
1987	0.6	−0.4630	(0.11)	0.4	−1.021	(0.12)

model, the 'ideal type' to which all others are compared (relative chances of 1.00) was a young person from social class I & II with five or more O grades in 1977.

First, we note that the relative chances of females with fathers in social class IIIn & IIIm having entered a 'reasonable job' in 1977 was significantly lower than for females from class I & II. For males the picture was rather different. Those with fathers in class IIIn & IIIm were more likely than those from class I & II to have entered a 'reasonable job', while those from class IV & V were marginally less likely. To test whether the influence of class on the chances of getting a 'reasonable job' had changed during the course of the decade, I added a class by year interaction to the model; it did not have a significant effect.

For both males and females qualifications are shown to have a powerful effect on the chances of entering a 'reasonable job', and relative chances were found to decline in line with qualifications. While the difference between males or females with five or more O grades and three or four O grades was relatively small, those with either one or two O grades or with no passes at grades A–C were at a significant disadvantage. Indeed, the chances of males with one or two O grades having entered a 'reasonable job' were half that of males with five or more O grades, while females with one or two O grades had their relative chances reduced by around 60 per cent. Those with no O grade passes had very little chance of entering a 'reasonable job', but the chances for males and females were similar.

The effects of social class and educational attainment are compounded by the effects of the decline in the youth labour market in different years. Thus in 1979 the relative chances of entering a 'reasonable job' declined by a factor of one for males and females, and continued to decline for much of the decade. Although the relative chances of males and females were similar in 1979, the decline in the youth labour market had a much more dramatic effect on females who saw their chances of obtaining 'reasonable jobs' halved in 1981. Opportunities for males did not fall as much and fell at a much slower pace.

The Unemployed

Any discussion of differential labour market outcomes over the decade up to 1987 must include a discussion of the effects of unemployment. However, it is difficult to compare unemployment rates of 17-year-olds in any meaningful sense due to the number of changes in the youth labour market. Youth schemes have grown from small beginnings to become a normal part of the transition of minimum-age school-leavers. They started as six month schemes, changing to a year duration and later to two years. In 1988 they became all but compulsory as benefits were withdrawn from young people who failed to join, but is probably fair to say that before 1988 it had become expected that unemployed young people would enter a scheme.

To make comparisons between young people who reported themselves as unemployed in either spring or autumn would have been misleading as the chances of a young person being unemployed was influenced by the availability of schemes and by their duration. Thus in 1977 a person who joined a scheme in the autumn might well have rejoined the ranks of the unemployed by spring. In 1987, with YTS extended to two years and with the threat of loss of benefit to those leaving without a job to go to, this might have been less likely.

In order to maintain some comparability, I confine myself to an examination of minimum-age school-leavers who were unemployed in the spring after school-leaving, who had not been on a work experience or training scheme and who had not had a job since leaving school. I shall refer to these as 'long-term unemployed': although in adult terms they would not be referred to as such, in terms of the majority of their peers this is an accurate description. From the 1977 questionnaires it is difficult to determine the long-term unemployed with any accuracy as it would have been possible for someone to have joined a scheme without it registering in the data. Because of this, I concentrate on the years 1979 to 1987.

The proportion of school-leavers who fell into this long-term unemployed category were relatively small in comparison to those unemployed at any one timepoint. Yet despite Government efforts over this period to eliminate long-term unemployment among school-leavers from the statistics, the continuously unemployed have doubled from 3 per cent in 1979 to 6 per cent in 1987 (Table 7.5).

Table 7.5: Minimum-age leavers continuously unemployed up to the spring, after leaving school; 1979 to 1987 (%)

	1979	1981	1983	1985	1987
	3%	3%	4%	5%	6%
Unweighted n (base)	(3756)	(3124)	(3704)	(3121)	(2113)

In order to assess the relative effects of class and qualifications on unemployment, in Table 7.6 I use a Logit model to examine the relative chances of long-term unemployment among minimum-age school-leavers in the spring after school-leaving. The ideal type against which comparisons were made is a young person from class I & II with five or more O grades in 1979 (relative chances of 1.00).

Table 7.6: Logit model predicting relative chances of minimum-age school-leavers being continuously unemployed up to the spring after leaving school (compared to social class I & II with five or more O grades in 1979)

	Male			Female		
	Relative chances	GLIM coefficient	(se)	Relative chances	GLIM coefficient	(se)
Class IIIn & IIIm	0.9	−0.1418	(0.19)	0.9	−0.06954	(0.20)
Class IV & V	1.1	0.1318	(0.20)	1.0	0.03092	(0.22)
3–4 O grades	0.9	−0.1391	(0.43)	0.6	−0.4575	(0.40)
1–2 O grades	1.5	0.3957	(0.35)	1.1	0.07052	(0.33)
No award/DE	2.8	1.033	(0.33)	2.0	0.6952	(0.30)
1981	0.7	−0.3308	(0.22)	1.3	0.2525	(0.21)
1983	1.3	0.2667	(0.19)	1.6	0.4681	(0.20)
1985	1.6	0.5015	(0.19)	1.9	0.6636	(0.20)
1987	1.8	0.5798	(0.20)	2.5	0.9186	(0.21)

In terms of social class, the differences in the relative chances of long-term unemployment were small and in both cases not statistically significant. The effects of social class were similar for males and females. In order to assess whether the effects of class on a young person's chances of long-term unemployment had changed over time, a class by year interaction was added to the model; the effect was not significant. This indicates that the effects of social class on the probability of long-term unemployment have not changed significantly since 1979.

However, important differences were found among young people with low qualifications. Males with no awards or 'fail grades' (D and E grades) were particularly vulnerable to long-term unemployment with relative chances nearly three times as great as those with five or more O grades. Females with no awards or 'fail grades' were twice as likely as those with five or more O grades to experience long-term unemployment. The relative chances of long-term unemployment also increased with time and became more serious for females. In 1987 young women's chances of long-term unemployment were around two-and-a-half times greater than in 1979, while young men's chances had increased by about 80 per cent.

In our discussion of the characteristics of the unemployed, we have confined the analysis to those who had been continuously unemployed by the spring after school-leaving. Many of these young people would have been scheme 'refusers' and it might have been more illuminating to examine the characteristics of 18- or 19-year-olds who were unemployed across time. To a large extent, we have been looking at the tip of the iceberg. In the 1980s, unemployment became an issue facing most young people. Even those who had no direct experience of unemployment made their plans within, and were faced with the constraints of, a society with high levels of unemployment. Despite the introduction of training schemes, the long-term unemployed school-leaver is still with us and showing no signs of disappearing.

Conclusion

The decade 1977 to 1987 was certainly a decade of decline for young people's prospects of employment. The old pattern in which a majority of school-leavers were in full-time employment soon after leaving school disappeared and a new transitional pattern emerged in which only a minority of young people were in employment six months after leaving school. In some parts of the country this would be a very small minority indeed. Thus the transition from school in the 1980s was characterized by widespread experience of unemployment and under-employment and increased participation in educa-tion, and training schemes. As far as minimum-age school-leavers are concerned these changes have brought few benefits.

However, despite these changes there were some similarities between 1977 and 1987. Throughout the decade it was young people with poor qualifications who suffered the worst effects of the recession. Those from the lower social classes often had an added disadvantage, although when I controlled for qualifications, I found that the effects of the recession had not greatly increased the vulnerability of young people from working-class homes. Despite the advances made by young people from the working classes in terms of qualifications, the links between education and social class remain strong. Those with poor qualifications were frequently young people from the working class.

Young people from the middle classes were not immune to the changes. Those who entered the labour market at the age of 16 found that their chances of prolonged unemployment had increased over much of the decade, and their chances of securing 'reasonable jobs' had declined, as had the chances of leavers from other social classes. In cases where young people from middle-class families 'fail' in the education system, their class background will do little to insulate them from the effects in the decline in the youth labour market.

Acknowledgments

The Scottish Young People's Survey is funded by the Scottish Education Department, the Industry Department for Scotland, the Training Agency (formely the MSC) and the Department of Employment. Work on the Trends data set was funded by the ESRC as part of its support for the CES as an ESRC Designated Research Centre. While I gratefully acknowledge the support given, the views expressed here are not necessarily shared by the sponsors.

I would like to thank David Raffe for his comments and advice on this paper and on an earlier draft, and also Gill Jones and Joan Payne for their helpful comments. I am also endebted to Cathy Garner and Lindsay Paterson for their help with Logit models and with the GLIM package.

From:- Youth in Transition

Claire Wallace + Malcolm Cross

Chapter 8

Class and Gender Divisions among Young Adults at Leisure

Ken Roberts, Rosemary Campbell and Andy Furlong

Introduction

Comparing peak with peak and trough with trough in successive business cycles, unemployment rose steadily in most parts of Britain during the late 1960s and 1970s. An even sharper rise occurred during the 1979–81 recession, and school-leavers proved the most vulnerable of all age-groups. Since the early 1980s unemployment among Britain's 16–18-year-olds has subsided, but the majority's former swift transitions from full-time education into full-time employment at the statutory school-leaving age have not been restored. Most 16–18-year-olds are now in various forms of education or training. Protracted transitions into the labour market have become the norm, and the following passages consider the implications for leisure of young adults' various experiences during the years immediately following their compulsory education. We shall show that whether 16-year-olds continue in education, obtain jobs, proceed through the Youth Training Scheme (YTS), or become unemployed makes a considerable difference to their leisure opportunities and behaviour, but that the effects are not exactly the same for males and females. Our evidence shows that young adults' new social condition, the limbo that many now experience between completing compulsory education and becoming established in employment, tends to widen social class disparities in life-styles, and that unemployment deepens traditional gender divisions.

In Scotland the types of young people following old and new pathways into the workforce have been monitored in a series of young people's surveys conducted biennially by Edinburgh University's Centre for Educational Sociology since 1977, though the 1983/4 fourth year cohort was the first group to be studied longitudinally through three mailed questionnaire sweeps tracing their progress in 1985, 1986 and 1987. The sample's leisure was studied only in the third, 1987 questionnaire survey when the average age of respondents was 19.25 years. However, information about respondents' backgrounds and biographies since completing compulsory education was collected in the earlier surveys, which means that the individuals' leisure behaviour in 1987 can be related not only to their circumstances at that time but also to their antecedent experiences. So as to derive maximum value from the space available for the questions on leisure and certain other items, the 1987 questionnaire was divided into two versions, each containing half of the relevant questions. This division produced a wide spread of information about the leisure activities, companions and group memberships of sufficient numbers of young adults not only to compare males with females, groups with different experiences in education, employment and unemployment, but to analyze the interactive implications of these divisions.

The original target sample for the 1984 fourth year cohort was 8,044 (10 per cent of the school year selected by birthdate) and the overall response rate to each survey was in the region of 80 per cent. In total, 4,013 individuals responded to all three sweeps, representing approximately 50 per cent of the original target sample. Response rates varied according to qualification levels, with higher response rates being achieved from those young people with the better educational qualifications. Throughout the survey, a variety of attrition-reduction methods were used to minimize the sample bias which can result from selective non-response (see Dodds *et al.*, 1989). However, the data from all the surveys has been weighted so that the resulting distributions of sample members match figures provided by the Scottish Education Department for fourth year Scottish Certificate of Education attainments by males and females. In the 1986 and 1987 surveys the weighting also took account of the distribution between early school-leavers and later leavers.

Several aspects of the sample's leisure were investigated in the 1987 survey, all using fully-structured questions. Individuals were asked to tick from checklists the types of people they spent time with when not busy, the number of evenings on which they 'went out' during a normal week, their frequencies of participation is a list of leisure activities (some common and others relatively rare), the types of groups that they belonged to, and their frequency of taking part in such 'organized' activities. Much of the following analysis compares respondents' involvement with specific types of groups, activities and companions. Then, in addition, respondents are compared according to the total number of different kinds of groups that they belonged to, the total number of leisure activities they engaged in, and their ranges and sources of leisure companionship. Also, the results of factor-analyses of respondents' participation in activities and groups are used to reveal the kinds of leisure behaviour that tended to accompany each other among different sections of the sample.

Gender Differences

None of the gender differences recorded in this research are particularly surprising. They simply confirm the findings of previous studies. More males were playing and watching sport, and placing bets, while more of the young women were going out for meals, reading books and magazines, going to cinemas, theatres, concerts and churches, and visiting friends and relatives. Some activities were equally popular or uncommon among both sexes. Going to pubs and discos, and listening to records were instances of the former, and visiting exhibitions, galleries and museums, attending trade union and political meetings, and doing voluntary work were examples of the latter.

In general, the Scottish women in our sample were not leading narrower leisure lives than the men. In fact the women had the slightly higher overall activity scores, calculated from their ranges and frequencies of participation. One might argue that the males' leisure was the more locked within a narrow masculine track dominated by sport and drink. The males were not the more active across leisure activities in general, though they did dominate in organized group leisure. The men reported an average of 1.01 voluntary association memberships compared with just 0.69 for the women. Fifty-seven per cent of the females belonged to no organizations against just 36 per cent of the men. This male lead was mainly, but not entirely, due to their more frequent sports club membership. Factor analysis of the sample's involvement in organized groups revealed three main clusters among both sexes, but in each case the males' clusters were the broader. Membership of social clubs tended to go along with participation in hobby clubs for both sexes, but the males who were involved in such groups also tended to belong to sports clubs. Memberships of religious and youth organizations were related, and, among males only, of drama and music groups. Political party and trade union membership tended to go together, but the males, unlike the females who belonged to such organizations, also tended to be members of social clubs.

We found, like all previous investigators, that the sexes were tending to operate in rather different kinds of leisure networks. Again there was a male tendency towards group leisure — informal group leisure in this case. The males were the more likely to be spending time in same-sexed and mixed-sex groups, whereas the females were the more likely to be spending time with their families, and in monosexual and heterosexual dyads. Every study throughout the history of youth (and adult) leisure research has shown that females' life-styles are the more home-based, and the majority of investigations have indicated that boys are the more likely to belong to 'gangs' or similar groups. Within our Scottish sample, the latter tendency was not entirely due to the females being 'ahead' in heterosexual development. Males with spouses or girl-friends were still more likely than females with equivalent partners to be spending some time in same-sexed groups, while the females were the more likely to be keeping up family relationships and their contacts with special same-sexed friends.

In general the females' life-styles were the more home-centred, and the males were going out on more evenings per week (3.7 on average, compared with 3.2 for the women). Nevertheless, the women were not the more isolated: the sexes were equally likely to report spending some time on their own. As already noted, the young women's ranges of leisure activity were, if anything, broader than the men's, and the females' leisure networks tended to include more types of companions — an average of 2.9 different sources compared with 2.7 for the men. The males were going out the more frequently, but tended to be locked into the rather narrower ranges of masculine activities and relationships.

Factor analysis of the sample's involvement in leisure activities revealed five main clusters, but their composition differed in significant ways between the males and females. The males' main clusters were:

    i Sport: playing, watching, and placing bets.
    ii Other out-of-home leisure: going out to cinemas, theatres, museums, exhibitions, and for meals.
    iii Home-based leisure: listening to tapes and records, reading books, and visiting relatives and friends.
    iv Domestic work: doing masculine and feminine jobs around the house.

v Civic activities: going to churches and religious meetings, and doing voluntary work.

The structure of the females' leisure was rather different, firstly in that playing and watching sport were not associated with betting but formed part of a much broader out-of-home leisure cluster. However, probably the most important difference of all was that, among the young women, the home-based leisure cluster incorporated feminine jobs around the house. When the males participated in home-based leisure such as listening to records, they were not necessarily doing more than that — indulging in pure leisure. In contrast, the women also tended to be undertaking domestic tasks in their homes. Deem (1986) has stressed how frequently adult women have to combine leisure activities with various forms of work, and our evidence suggests that Scotland's female teenagers are still being prepared for such leisure futures.

Students, Workers and the Unemployed

Some of the differences between the men's and women's leisure may have been merely that — just differences — rather than advantages and disadvantages, but this could hardly be said of the contrasts between our respondents who were still in full-time education, in full-time jobs, and unemployed. In almost every respect the students were the most leisure-privileged, while the unemployed were the most deprived. The students had the highest overall level of recreational activity due to their greater involvement in playing sport, reading, going to cinemas, theatres, concerts, exhibitions, galleries, museums and churches, and for meals out. There were only two kinds of leisure where respondents in jobs were the most active — watching sport and betting. The students had the highest rate of organized group membership. Indeed, they held a clear lead with every kind of group except trade unions. The students also had the broadest social networks reporting an average of 3.2 sources of companionship against 2.7 for both the employed and unemployed. The students were the most likely to report spending some of their time with same-sexed groups, mixed groups, individual friends of the same sex, and on their own. The only instances of other respondents deriving more companionship from any source were the employed's greater likelihood of having opposite-sexed boy-friends or girl-friends, and the unemployed's greater involvement with their families. Yet despite their wider ranges of leisure activity and group memberships, and their broader social networks, the students were the most likely to report spending some time on their own, and 'went out' on the fewest number of evenings per week. Previous investigations dating back to the 1940s have noted this extraordinary time-pressure with which academic young people learn to cope (Ward, 1948; Prosser, 1981).

It is noteworthy that the students' leisure was relatively rich in both masculine and feminine spheres. Their high participation in cultural fields and in same-sexed dyads, and their broad-based social networks were general features of females' leisure. However, the students were also the most involved in masculine pastimes such as playing sport, formal organizations, and informal group-based leisure. In contrast, all the areas where employed respondents' leisure was the richest — number of evenings out, watching (but not playing) sport, and betting — were characteristic of male rather than female life-styles. The gender-neutrality of the leisure returns from remaining in full-time education, compared with the male bias in the advantages of immediate employment could be among the reasons for females' higher stay-on rates in schools and colleges beyond the statutory leaving-age which have been recorded in research in all parts of the United Kingdom.

Our finding that the unemployed's leisure was the most impoverished will surprise no-one familiar with previous studies. These have explained how and why most of its young victims find unemployment 'an ordeal' (Hendry *et al.*, 1984). They spend enormous amounts of time just 'hanging about' (Kelly and Raymond, 1988; Roberts, Brodie and Dench, 1987), and may regress socially and psychologically (Furlong and Spearman, 1989; Gurney, 1980). In our survey the unemployed were 'going out' on more evenings per week than the students, but on fewer occasions than individuals with jobs. The unemployed had the lowest rates of participation in a wide range of masculine and feminine activities — watching sport, playing sport, going to cinemas, theatres, concerts, exhibitions, galleries, museums, churches, pubs, discos, trade union and political meetings, and for meals out. The kinds of leisure where the unemployed's participation equalled the employed's make a much shorter list — betting, reading, voluntary work, and visits to friends and families. Organizational membership among the unemployed stood at only half the rate for respondents in jobs. The unemployed's social networks were as broad-based as employees', but the former's were more likely to include family members, and less likely to include opposite-sexed boy- and girl-friends, and groups of any composition. The unemployed were also more likely than the employed, though less likely than students, to report spending some time on their own.

The fact that the students were the leisure-rich group suggests that spending power cannot be the sole factor on which young adults' access to leisure depends, though it is a mistake to imagine that post-compulsory students are always disadvantaged financially. Spending power depends not only on current, but also on anticipated future income. In any case, many students have part-time or temporary jobs, and on entering higher education they become eligible for (means-tested) grants. In this survey the students had higher average weekly incomes, just over £40, than the unemployed, just under £30. The individuals in jobs, with average personal incomes of around £80 per week, had by far the most cash to spend. However, the students had the advantage of tending to be drawn from the more privileged families, who often provide not only cash but access to a wide range of leisure equipment. In 1987 the ESRC 16–19 Initiative found that 18-year-old students were more likely to have the use of motor cars than same-aged peers in full-time jobs (Roberts and Parsell, 1988a). Students have further leisure advantages, including a still generally-esteemed role with which to identify. Also, their educational institutions normally offer a wide range of free or heavily-subsidized sports, social and cultural facilities, and students are in daily contact with other members of their age-group, mostly with similar sources and levels of income, and recreational tastes. The unemployed have none of these assets, and they lack the incomes of individuals in employment.

Many of the 'social class' differences in young adults' leisure recorded in Scotland in 1987 have very long histories. For instance, ever since information has been collected the academically successful have been the most frequent sport participants, and the most active in most kinds of recreational organizations. Working-class leisure has always been relatively informal (Hargreaves, 1967). However, until the 1970s there were sound reasons for describing academically-dedicated pupils, especially those who stayed on beyond the statutory leaving-age, as 'deferring gratification'. In the 1950s and 60s involvement in youth culture was associated with educational failure (Coleman, 1961; Sugarman, 1967). Commercial youth cultures spread first among affluent young wage-earners, and it took some time before pop scenes invaded Britain's grammar schools and colleges. Recent evidence, including our Scottish findings, questions whether any truth remains in the old idea of post-compulsory students sacrificing immediate leisure satisfactions. Rather than contrasting students' and out-of-school youth's different *levels* of involvement in youth culture, it appears to make greater sense today to talk of different groups becoming involved in different young adult life-styles. And according to our evidence, these life-styles correspond closely to the educational or labour market careers that the age-group follows.

The Longer-term Leisure-effects of Education and Unemployment

An advantage in adding leisure questions to the Scottish Young People's Survey in 1987 lies in the sheer wealth of contextual information that was being, and had already been, gathered about the sample's current situations, family backgrounds and histories since their secondary school days. This enables us to test whether the effects of post-compulsory education and early unemployment experiences were confined to the young adults' leisure at the time, or whether there were longer-lasting traces.

Table 8.1 divides the sample into those who were still in full-time education at the time of the 1987 survey (mainly in higher education), those who had left after completing the fifth or sixth years, and minimum-age leavers. The two latter groups are then sub-divided according to whether they were employed or unemployed at the time of the enquiry. The five groups thus distinguished are then compared on the four summary measures of leisure participation being used throughout this analysis — their overall levels of activity, the breadth of their social networks, their organizational memberships, and the number of evenings when they 'went out' in a typical week. On all indicators except evenings out the individuals who were still in full-time education had the highest scores, followed by the older, then the minimum-age leavers. However, among both the older and minimum-age leavers, the respondents currently in jobs had higher leisure activity and group membership scores than the unemployed, while with current status held constant the older leavers had consistently higher scores on all three indicators. This suggests that the leisure relationships and activities fostered during post-compulsory education are retained, and enrich individuals' leisure after they have entered the labour market. Our evidence cannot prove or disprove that such effects are life-long. It is clear that post-compulsory education was not protecting the sample against the disadvantages inflicted by subsequent unemployment. However, the advantages of post-compulsory education were evident whether individuals were currently employed or unemployed, and were obviously lasting at least into young adulthood.

Table 8.2 divides the sample into those with less and more than a year's experience of unemployment, then splits each of these groups according to whether they were in full-time education, jobs, or unemployed at the time of the investigation. Among those with little if any exposure to unemployment, the students had the highest scores on all the leisure indicators except evenings out, while the employed outscored the unemployed in general levels of leisure activity and group membership. Among those with longer experience of unemployment, having obtained jobs or returned to education by the time of the enquiry was raising levels of general leisure activity and organizational membership, but education did not appear to be having its normal broadening

Table 8.1: Length of time in education and leisure

Current status	Still in educ.	Older leavers		Minimum-age leavers	
		Job	Unempl.	Job	Unempl.
Mean Scores					
Overall leisure activity	22.0	21.3	19.1	19.2	17.3
Sources of companions	3.3	2.8	2.9	2.6	2.6
Group membership	1.2	1.0	0.6	0.8	0.3
Number of evenings out per week	2.8	3.7	3.2	3.8	3.2
N	517	476	71	491	110

Table 8.2: Past experience of unemployment and leisure

Current status	Less than one year unemployed			One year or longer unemployed		
	Educ.	Job	Unempl.	Educ.	Job	Unempl.
Mean Scores						
Overall leisure activity	22.3	19.8	19.2	19.5	19.3	17.6
Sources of companions	3.2	2.6	2.8	2.5	2.4	2.7
Group membership	1.09	0.86	0.50	0.85	0.78	0.45
Number of evenings out per week	3.3	3.7	3.2	2.6	3.4	3.3
N	64	333	64	24	63	105

Table 8.3: YTS experience and leisure

Current status	Been on YTS		Not been on YTS	
	Employed	Unemployed	Employed	Unemployed
Mean Scores				
Overall leisure activity	19.72	17.40	20.33	17.69
Sources of companions	2.59	2.48	2.73	2.78
Group membership	0.79	0.35	0.90	0.42
Group activity	4.48	4.00	4.48	4.69
Number of evenings out per week	3.89	3.35	3.64	3.17
N	517	155	591	145

effects on their social networks. Moreover, the depressing effects of previous unemployment were still evident in the levels of leisure activity and group membership of those who had subsequently obtained jobs or resumed full-time studies. These enduring scars of unemployment were as vivid in our evidence as the longer-term benefits of post-compulsory education.

Interestingly, the longer-term leisure-effects of having been on the Youth Training Scheme (YTS) were more akin to those of unemployment than post-compulsory education. With current status controlled, all the sub-groups that had *never* been on schemes had the higher general leisure activity and group membership scores, and the wider social networks (see Table 8.3). Training schemes rarely offer the same recreational facilities as education institutions. Trainees' incomes are closer to the young unemployed's than same-aged workers'. There is independent evidence of the status, time-structuring and activity-promoting aspects of youth training averting the decline in psychological well-being that otherwise tends to occur when young people become unemployed (Banks and Ullah, 1988; Furlong and Spearman, 1989). However, according to our evidence the benefits of the YTS do not extend into leisure socialization.

Middle-class family backgrounds were associated with the same rich leisure patterns as post-compulsory education, and the influence of their home backgrounds was still evident in 1987 whether individuals were then in full-time education, employment, or unemployed. With current situations held constant, those from middle-class families always had the wider social networks, and the highest levels of general leisure activity and group membership. The sum of the above evidence, therefore, suggests that individuals have leisure careers in which successive experiences make the same kinds of cumulative and enduring impressions as episodes and attainments during careers in education and jobs. Just as the potential vocational benefits of early educational success are never entirely erased, so the advantages of a childhood in a family that offers a wealth of leisure experiences appear to be carried into adulthood whatever the individuals' subsequent experiences. However, adults do not simply enact leisure programmes learnt as children. Their leisure careers develop. They can acquire or lose interests and relationships, at least temporarily, when enabled or constrained by subsequent circumstances. And like family backgrounds, the influences that make an impression on individuals' leisure during subsequent life-phases are traceable into later stages of their leisure careers. Neither the relatively rich leisure of the full-time students, nor the relatively impoverished leisure of the unemployed in our sample could be attributed entirely to their current circumstances. Nevertheless, these situations were having clear effects on the individuals' leisure that appeared likely to outlast the circumstances that were responsible.

Now it is well known that, generally speaking, middle-class family backgrounds are associated with educational success and entry to higher education, just as working-class origins are associated with relatively modest attainments at school and, during recent years in many cases, with early labour market difficulties. So the leisure-learning that occurs during the years immediately following compulsory education will normally operate as one set of links in a longer-term process of socio-cultural reproduction whereby class-based life-styles are transmitted down the generations. Leisure learning during this life-phase will also feature among the processes of socialization through which those who are already educationally, and potentially occupationally mobile, can be socially assimilated into the strata they are joining.

Class Differences in a Gender Context

In most respects the leisure-implications of class positions were gender-neutral, but there were some specific ways in which male and female leisure were being affected differently by the individuals' class locations. In all these instances the females were deriving the greater benefits, relative to other members of their own sex, by remaining in full-time education, and were suffering relatively heavy leisure penalties during unemployment. Leaving education, even for full-time employment, was associated with much steeper declines among females than among males in sports participation (68 per cent to 38 per cent compared with 78 to 71 per cent) and group memberships (averages of 1.03 and 0.63 for female students and employees, compared with 1.11 and 1.05 for males). Also, rather than being less affected by unemployment, the females' leisure was being curtailed the more sharply in the sense of making the greater difference to their frequency of 'going out'. Unemployed females were going out on 2.80 evenings per week on average compared with 3.54 among those in jobs, whereas the comparable figures for males were 3.68 and 3.97. Unemployment was increasing other family members' prominence in both sexes' social networks, but especially among the females. Previous researchers have noted how frequently unemployment confines young females within domestic settings (Griffin, 1985; Willis, 1985). The unemployed males in our sample were the more likely to be continuing to 'go out' in the evenings even when they did not appear to be taking part in any approved or even recognized forms of recreation.

Class divisions were making broadly the same kinds of differences to males' and females' leisure, but among females these differences were somewhat wider, which confirms our earlier observation that, for females, the leisure rewards of continuing in full-time education will be especially attractive. Correspondingly, from the point of view of defending their general quality of life, the young women in our sample appeared to be at the greater risk of damage from unemployment.

Gender Divisions in Different Class Contexts

In general, the same gender differences in leisure practices were present whether we compared 19-year-old males and females in education, jobs or unemployed. The females always had the wider networks because they were the more likely to spend time with their families, in same-sexed dyads, and in heterosexual partnerships. Males were always the more likely to belong to same-sexed groups, were going out on the greater number of evenings per week, and had the highest rates of organized group membership. In contrast, the females in all social classes had the broader ranges of leisure activity, and the slightly higher overall scores for leisure participation. Males were always the more likely to play and watch sport, and to bet, whereas the females were consistently the more likely to have meals out, and to attend churches, cinemas, and concerts. Whether they were in full-time education, jobs or unemployed, the sexes' rates of attendance at pubs and discos were virtually identical.

However, certain gender differences were narrowest among the students. Sport participation was one example. Group membership rates, and frequency of going out in the evenings, were further instances. Also, males and females in full-time education were equally likely to spend time in mixed-sex groups, whereas this type of companionship was more common among employed and unemployed males than among their female counterparts. Gender inequalities in evenings out and group membership rates were widest among the unemployed.

Within full-time education there was a convergence of male and female leisure patterns on account of the women closing the gaps in certain areas where males generally dominated. Among the employed and unemployed, in contrast, any convergence between males' and females' leisure was occurring for rather different reasons. Employed and unemployed females' participation rates in certain spheres where their own sex normally led — visits to cinemas, concerts, exhibitions and other cultural events — declined towards and sometimes beneath their male counterparts' levels. Meanwhile, employed and unemployed males were retaining their 'normal' leads in areas where males generally dominated the leisure scenes, especially in sport and group leisure.

Male and female students were certainly not following identical leisure patterns. However, gender differences among the students were narrower than among other young adults. Within student cultures, masculine and feminine life-styles were overlapping at high participation levels in informal and group-based leisure, and in the sense of both sexes being involved in broad-based social networks.

There has been a general trend in recent decades towards closing and even eradicating some former sex differences in leisure behaviour. For example, the gap between men's and women's sports participation rates has narrowed. In this Scottish research the females were as regular visitors to pubs and discos as males in all social classes. We doubt whether this would have been found even as recently as the 1970s. However, our evidence suggests that gender divisions at leisure have become narrowest of all among young adults who remain in full-time post-compulsory education. Insofar as the students' leisure remained gender divided, it would be as easy to construct an argument for females as for males being the relatively advantaged sex. In contrast, our earlier claim to have recorded sex differences rather than inequalities must be considered more controversial in relation to subjects who were employed, and most difficult to sustain in respect of the unemployed.

A Domestic Solution?

Previous investigators have explained how youth unemployment bars its victims from conventional and respectable routes through engagement and marriage towards new household and family formation (Wallace, 1987a; Willis, 1985). Young unemployed couples cannot afford to save for deposits on houses, or even for home furnishings. Post-compulsory students are in similar situations, except that they have far better long-term occupational prospects and, according to our evidence, immediate leisure gratifications, which must operate as inducements to postpone marriage and parenthood. The absence of such compensations could be a reason why the young unemployed are less prudent. All the relevant enquiries have found the young unemployed entering marital or cohabiting relationships, and becoming parents, ahead of other groups. Since the 1970s, throughout Britain, there have been slight rises in the mean ages of first marriages and when women first become mothers. However, females are still experiencing these life-events ahead of males, and traditional class differences are persisting. The middle classes still delay, while working-class young adults make relatively early transitions to adult domestic roles (Dunnell, 1976).

Our 19-year-olds who were in jobs or unemployed were more likely to be engaged than full-time students. This applied among males (10.9 and 10.4 against 1.3 per cent) and females (19.6 and 18.1 against 5.6 per cent). However, in terms of already having embarked upon cohabitation or marital relationships, it was the young unemployed who stood apart. Of all females who were neither in jobs nor full-time education, 16.7 per cent were living with opposite-sexed partners compared with 4.0 per cent of those in employment and just 0.8 per cent of the students. Among males the equivalent figures were 5.6, 2.8 and 1.4 per cent. Just under 5 per cent of unemployed males had children compared with 2.0 per cent of those in jobs, and 0.2 per cent of the students. Among the females the equivalent figures were 21.6, 0.5 and 0.2 per cent. The 19-year-old female students and employees were no more likely to have already become parents than males in similar positions, but the females who were not employed were far more likely than both their male equivalents and other young women to have become mothers.

We have seen that unemployment inflicts especially severe leisure deprivations on young women. So it becomes tempting to construct an argument attributing teenage fertility among unemployed females to motherhood offering an escape from, and a solution to, the problems of joblessness. However, the sum of our evidence will not sustain this argument. It seemed that their fertility had removed the young mothers from employment rather than their inability to obtain jobs somehow having influenced them to become pregnant. Fifty-nine per cent of females who had children but no jobs at the time of the survey had held at least one job at some time in the past, whereas only 51 per cent of unemployed childless women had been employed previously. These two groups of non-employed females — those with children and those without — had very similar prior experiences in terms of the duration of their unemployment: 67 and 64 per cent had been unemployed for over a year in total since leaving school.

Our evidence confirms that teenage motherhood is most common among working-class early school-leavers who fail to, or never try to, obtain 'good jobs'; but this has been the case for generations, throughout the post-war decades of full employment. Westwood (1984) has illustrated how the prospect of a domestic life-style can appear especially attractive to women working in dull, repetitive, unskilled jobs. It promises an escape from the monotony of working life, although the reality of looking after a family can be rather different. However, the relatively low employment rate among our young mothers seemed to be due entirely to their domestic situations having led to their withdrawal from the labour market, rather than their opting for domesticity as a result of especially severe employment difficulties. Moreover, motherhood was obviously intensifying rather than offering an escape from the leisure restrictions associated with female unemployment. The young mothers' life-styles were more domesticated, and more dominated by family relationships than any other groups'. The mothers were the group most likely to name other family members, opposite-sexed partners and children as sources of companionship, but they were the least likely to name same-sexed friends, or to belong to either same-sexed or mixed-sexed groups. Only 9 per cent of the housewives belonged to any formal leisure organizations — far fewer even than among other unemployed females. The housewives were more likely than any other group of females to bet, and to report visiting kin and friends. They also went out for meals more frequently than other unemployed females, and were more likely than both the employed and unemployed to attend churches. However, the housewives had the lowest participation rates in playing and watching sport, reading, listening to records, going to pubs, cinemas, theatres, concerts, cultural events and places, and voluntary work. Rather than opening new leisure horizons, teenage motherhood was clearly imposing exceptionally tight boundaries around the recreation of those concerned.

Conclusions

Childhood and youth are life-phases during which most individuals acquire the leisure capital on which they trade for the rest of their lives (Boothby *et al.*, 1981; Hantrais and Kamphorst, 1987). Adult leisure tends to be built on, or drawn from, repertoires established when young. In so far as leisure contributes to the general quality of life in our society, the policy implications of the findings presented above as regards provisions for the 16–19 age-group seem crystal clear. In terms of the quality of their present and future leisure, it is clearly disadvantageous for young people to experience unemployment, especially prolonged unemployment, and even more so for these same young people to make early transitions to adult domestic roles. From the point of view of leisure socialization, full-time post-compulsory education was conferring greater benefits even than full-time employment, and was far preferable to periods in youth training. Also, full-time education appeared more conducive to sex equality at leisure than any other milieux. At present in Britain, the different kinds of protracted transitions into the labour market which young people experience will be tending to perpetuate class divisions at leisure. The benefits of expanding educational opportunities, in addition to any vocational returns, will include a narrowing of sex and class divisions in leisure practices not just among young people, but also, insofar as the effects are lasting, throughout the adult population of the future.

Acknowledgment

The evidence in this article is from the Scottish Young People's Survey which is funded by the Scottish Education Department, the Industry Department for Scotland, the Training Agency, and the Department of Employment. While the authors gratefully acknowledge the support given, the views expressed here are not necessarily shared by the sponsors of the survey.

Chapter 9

Creating Poverty and Creating Crime:
Australian Youth Policy in the Eighties

Mike Presdee

Since coming to power in 1983 the Australian Labor Government, under the prime ministership of Bob Hawke, has struggled to produce a comprehensive and coherent set of youth policies to which the Government could be genuinely committed. After the 1984 elections, when young people deserted the Labor party in droves, the Prime Minister launched his Government's 'solution' to the 'youth problem' which took the form of a policy package called 'Priority One — Young Australia'. This package contained a number of elements, from the introduction of work 'traineeships' to campaigns to deal with drug abuse. The most prominent element of Priority One, however, was a massive publicity campaign launched by the Prime Minister himself. Advertisements, leaflets, radio and television coverage were all used to saturate the community with the message that young people were to be 'seen, heard, educated, encouraged, trained, employed, housed and treated as the future of this country'. This type of 'feel good' propaganda campaign was characteristic of the United Nations International Year of Youth approach to youth issues also in 1985. It also provided the context for the Prime Minister to embark upon a campaign which was unprecedented in recent times in Australia.

Under the banner of 'Priority One', Bob Hawke criss-crossed Australia in an effort to let young people 'have their say' by speaking about their concerns. Toll-free telephone numbers were advertised, talkback radio shows featuring the Prime Minister arranged, and rock concerts starring Bob Hawke (and Molly Meldrum, compere of the popular ABC TV music show *Countdown*) along with popular musicians were set up. According to the Government's figures, some 26,000 young Australians used this opportunity to convey their messages directly to the Prime Minister and his Government. All up, the cost of the advertising campaign and the phone-in was around one and a half million dollars. To further emphasize his commitment to the young people of Australia, Hawke moved the Office of Youth Affairs into the Department of the Prime Minister and Cabinet and assumed the responsibility for Youth Affairs. The newly discovered 'commitment' and 'priority' being given to young people was replicated at the State level in many instances as well. In South Australia, for example, the Bannon Labor Government created a new Cabinet position — the Minister for Youth Affairs — in 1985.

In reality it was the Labor Party needing a youth policy that was the priority, rather than youth themselves being made a priority. The substance of the policy itself contained all the old programmes, updated and refined, wrapped up in the rhetoric of self-improvement and, as such, was doomed to failure (Presdee and White, 1987).

Since then the Labor Government has continued to review its 'youth strategy', and responsibility for youth affairs has been moved away from the Prime Minister's department, first to the education ministry, and now to the Minister for Employment and Education Services, Peter Duncan. In October 1988 this new minister announced yet another review of policy which was supposed to result in 'social justice for youth'. This is the new political catch-phrase that will masquerade as the cornerstone for youth policy in the 90s, whilst the same intervention policies, aimed at corralling young people into employment, education and training programmes, will progress unhindered. It is these policies, under the rhetoric of a guarantee of employment, education or training for all young people, that have become a focus for policy makers. Realizing that they have been unable to finance such a guarantee they have created policies that in practice resulted in the coercion of young people into education and training by the removal of subsistence allowances, and that have forced thousands of young Australians into poverty, on to the streets, and into crime.

Labor Market Programmes

For ten years various Australian Governments have developed a smorgasbord approach to education and labor market programmes that have fallen into five broad categories:

1   *Assistance to employers who offer apprenticeships*
    e.g. Commonwealth Rebate for Apprentice Full-time Training (CRAFT)
2   *Direct wage subsidy payments to employers*
    e.g. Special Youth Employment Training Program (SYETP)
    — later replaced by 'Jobstart' in 1985
3   *Short-term employment programme for 'disadvantaged' unemployed people*
    e.g. Community Employment Program (CEP)
4   *Improving the job skills and 'life skills' of young people*
    e.g. School to Work Transition Program
    Education Program for Unemployed Youth (EPUY)
    Community Youth Support Scheme (CYSS)
    Skill Share Program (1988)
5   *Integrated on-and-off the job vocational training*
    e.g. Australian Traineeship System (ATS)
    A combination of structured on-the-job training and Technical and Further Education training (TAFE)
    Job Train (for long term unemployed) 1988
    Job Search 1988

The Experience of Young People

As the rift widens between how the Government thinks people live and the everyday reality that many experience, so the belief intensifies that improvements in training opportunities and schooling, will, on their own, persuade young unemployed people to give up their so-called 'hedonistic' lives of leisure and suspend their involvement in the enterprise culture of affluence, whilst they are re-trained and re-schooled, ready for life on the dole at 18 rather than 16.

The 'offer' of a reduction in income by the removal of social security for 16- and 17-year-olds, in November 1987, was one that a great number of young people were always likely to reject, forcing even more young people to attempt to survive a consumer society in conditions of poverty. As Frank Maas has suggested, the policy proposals introduced in the 1988 May economic statement 'seem destined to exacerbate rather than reduce problems such as family conflict and young homelessness' and, we might add, increase crime

(Maas, 1988). The present situation points significantly to disaster when we consider that in January 1988 there were 60,000 16- and 17-year-olds 'not at school, not at a tertiary institution' and looking for work (Australian Bureau of Statistics, 1988). But the Social Services in Canberra had, on 29 January, given only 25,126 job search allowances, which rose only slightly to 26,055 on 11 March, clearly at a time when young people had already re-enrolled at school. Even allowing for the vagaries of statistical sampling techniques and the new thirteen week waiting period for 'dole' eligibility, there was still a staggering 30,000 plus young people without work, without a wage and without income. It is little wonder that the Human Rights Commissioner Burdekin, in his report on Australian young people released in February 1989, reported: '[Australian] . . . homeless children and homeless people are dying in some cases and suffering abuses of their rights in many others'; and the Minister in charge of youth affairs Peter Duncan responded

> There are already on the streets 25,000 of them [homeless youth] —
> *realistically double that.* And many of those who are not on the streets
> are dropping out of school, looking for jobs, or just standing in the
> unemployment queues waiting for handouts (*Sunday Mail* 19 March
> 1989).

There seems to have been a naive assumption, even though all the evidence shows otherwise, that all young people live happily at home, with parents who not only care but, more importantly, are competent and cope. Social policies that rely for their success on business practices such as money incentives or disincentives, have the potential to create casualties that could prove even more costly in the long run. Unlike business, human services cannot simply 'write-off' those that are no longer needed, or take to the scrap-heap the inefficient bits of humanity that seem unable to fit the new systems.

Youth Reponses: Social Absenteeism, Unemployment and Crime

In an attempt to gain greater understanding of the reactions of young people to the restructuring of their lives I undertook a series of investigations into the everyday lives of unemployed young people in Adelaide (a city of approximately 1.25 million people in South Australia).

1 Young people from the northern suburbs of Adelaide were closely interviewed.

2 Workers with youth, in a number of settings, had 'case studies' of young people who had been helped by their agency.

3 Ten 'street' youth had been interviewed.

4 A group of twenty young women involved in a special 'at risk' project in a northern suburbs high school were interviewed.

5 The November 1988 Adelaide youth phone-in project was especially designed to question young people about the effects of the new job-search allowance.

The official extent of juvenile crime in South Australia and the connection with unemployment has been well documented by the South Australian Office of Crime Statistics. The figures for the period 1 January — 30 June 1986 reveal a 3.4 per cent increase compared with the previous six months. Of 4,856 appearances the great majority were for relatively minor crimes, such as shop theft (57.9 per cent), breaking and entering (11.6 per cent) and offences against order (9.2 per cent). Under 1 per cent of all juvenile appearances involves an offence defined by the Department of Community Welfare researchers as a crime of violence; 46.2 per cent of young people appearing before courts were unemployed, whereas 72.3 per cent in front of juvenile aid panels were in the student/apprentice category. (Aid panels are composed of psychologists, social workers and lay people and are designed to divert young people away from the courts and from acquiring a criminal record.)

The situation for young women 'offenders' is worse than that of young men, with 55 per cent of young women 'offenders' being unemployed, compared to 45 per cent of young men. The figure for 15- and 16-year-old 'young women unemployed offenders' was dramatically high, being 68 per cent and 70 per cent, with the corresponding figure for young men being 48 per cent and 54 per cent.

The stress on young unemployed women is quite clear, as those without dole payments figure highly in the 'offenders' figures — precisely the conditions that the present Government has created for thousands more Australian youth.

The high unemployment areas of the outer western, southern and northern suburbs of Adelaide account for almost 70 per cent of all offences dealt with by the children's court, with the regional area of Elizabeth (part of

Adelaide) making up 36.6 per cent of the total. This, coupled with a high frequency 'court and panel appeareance' rate of 42.7 per 1000 Elizabeth and 51 per cent per 1000 Port Adelaide (against 4.6 for the middle-class eastern suburbs area of St Peters) shows clearly the class nature of criminalization. (It is not my intention here to discuss the added problem of race that faces, for example, the city of Elizabeth, but we should be aware of the over-representation of Aboriginals in all the figures, especially young Aboriginal women.)

The fact that the greater number of panel appearances are from young people still at school is little comfort when we consider the state of absenteeism still in schools, and the statistical connection between absenteeism and crime. The increasing number of truants shows the extent of the failure of present educational policies (especially for working-class young people), as 15-year-olds choose unemployment without the dole, over the unexciting learning environment of school and further education. There has been a continuing failure, by politicians, bureaucrats and academics in understanding the effects that schooling has on a vast number of young people, who have struggled not just with the content of the curriculum but with the very nature of the institutional form of schooling itself that stands as an instrument held over and against them. The cultural effects of being actively a part of something that you don't understand, and can't understand, is layered into the structures of everyday life, layered down in the minutiae of social interaction and social response so that it becomes difficult to separate out questions of class, race and gender. The sheer human pain of being powerless and unknowing, of being a confused recipient instead of an active participant, is rarely fully understood, as young people, early in their primary schooling, begin to learn their place in society and begin to respond accordingly. There is little surprise then that working-class children vote with their feet when given more of the same.

As one worker with youth pleaded:

Worker   How do you get a kid into a training programme who can neither read nor write, a kid that hasn't been to school since they were 7 years of age? They have played truant, the system has never been able to find something that is applicable to them. When they turn 15, miraculously they can read and write? No way! No way! They have lived out on the streets for donkey's yonks going from foster family into care, to out on the streets, to the Salvos, God knows where — they've been all round the place, they've never had the chance to stop and learn, and they don't want to, some of them, that's the other thing, you've got to get back to that choice stuff, you can't take choice away from a human being, it's almost an existential argument isn't it, because if they choose not to choose they still make a choice.

Interviewer   But aren't we dealing here with just a small minority of young people?

Worker   What's a small minority, I mean, uh, between 15–19? When you consider my major client group is 15–19 years, I see forty kids a week in that age group of which a percentage would probably be — oh 2 per cent would be at school, it's a joke, it's not a minority, I'm talking about majorities here, I'm talking about kids that — in the month of July I saw six 10–14-year-olds; a hundred and sixteen 15–19-year-olds; thirty-eight 20–24-year-olds and a hundred and fifteen mums and dads, you tell me, and of those 7 per cent were at school, it's a hoot.

Without exception, all young unemployed people that were interviewed had truanted from school at some time, beginning an early pattern of 'offending'. Truanting was a response to problems faced within the school, with young people rarely truanting to do specific things, but simply to steal both time and space for themselves in which they could for a short period be autonomous, be free and be themselves, thus escaping — even for a short period of time — the rules, regulations and regimentation of schooling.

Young non-attenders have become the conscientious objectors of the education system. This is not the aggressive brick through the window nor the setting fire to schools. Rather, this is a passive withdrawal from a situation that hurts. Young people are more and more rejecting school because school has rejected them. Yet the removal of the dole underlines the Government's obsession with coercing young people into schools, come what may, without ever considering that schooling can and does create and perpetuate inequalities and that for many young people to be 'retained' in schools for longer necessitates fundamental changes in school organization, curriculum and power structures that have never seriously been contemplated.

There is little doubt that the rates of absenteeism are increasing in South Australia, with attendance officers reporting an increasing problem. The pattern and reasons are complex, but there are significant differences in daily rates between working-class schools such as Port Adelaide at 6.9 per cent, and middle-class schools such as Marryatville with just 1.7 per cent. The latest study undertaken by the Adelaide regional office estimates that 8,500 students are absent for more than one term a year and that on any one day 18,000 children may be absent for a variety of reasons. It is clear that a great majority of these would be absent with parental knowledge although not necessarily under the direct supervision and care of parents.

Young women are more often absent than young men, a pattern that starts in the late primary school and becomes exceptionally marked in year ten.

However, it is when young 15-year-olds, especially young women, finally leave school that the battle for income, for survival, begins in earnest. It appears that no matter how hard they try, in the end the way in which an income is achieved matters less and less. In each of my interviews every young person had broken some legal regulation, in some way, in their fight for survival. Although most had never been caught, they had, between them been guilty of:

Non-attendance at school
Vandalism
Drug use
Under-age carnal knowledge
Drinking
Smoking
Breaking and entering
Shop lifting
Prostitution
Driving offences
Non-declaration of taxable income

Sue: I'd left school and I wasn't on the dole and wasn't getting any money whatsoever. So I had to get some money somehow — from friends, borrowed from friends, hassle kids at the shops — not bash them, just give us your money or we're going to get you into so much trouble.

Ann: I used to steal out of Mum's purse all the time — if I went to a friend's place, I'd steal out of their Mum's purse. I just need the money. Mum would buy me a packet of smokes. I just had to have the money.

Rod: I'd been to court for just pinching . . . flogging stuff. It was cause I liked them, it was for my bike, a pair of pedals. I was with my two mates but they never knew I done it.

The extent that 'subsistence crime' is increasingly becoming a part of the lives of non-'street' young people was examined through the confidential phone-in weekend. All but two of those questioned were in the wealth-less under 18 years category, and out of a total of forty-three, 55 per cent were receiving the reduced job-search allowance of $25 (about £12) whilst 18 per cent received no income at all.

The most important factor of the phone-in was that 68 per cent of those interviewed were from stable homes, having lived for some time with one or both parents or a relative. They were not from that group of young people whose lives were in such confusion that they were without homes and families. These young people were living out the beginnings of adult life from a position of poverty, knowing that they could neither face, nor enter, in an acceptable way, any part of the education and training system. The pressures on relationships that resulted from being both unemployed and without subsistence confronted and consumed their everyday life, posing the single most important problem of their social existence. At a time when they were at their most vulnerable they were rendered both useless and wageless and were unable to form relationships from any position of status and autonomy. Nearly 70 per cent of those interviewed stated they had problems with families and friends, created by being wageless, whilst 54 per cent had problems created by being jobless.

Already over 50 per cent of this sample were committing crimes in order to subsist, involving breaking and entering, drug dealing, begging, prostitution and working in the cash economy. With relationships under stress all around them, these young people are 'at risk' of becoming homeless, defenceless and exploited. The conditions in which they now exist contain all the ingredients of human tragedy on a grand scale, that could, with a more flexible policy, be avoided. It is not enough to give help when the young become homeless, when relationships have already broken down — what is needed are policies that recognize the needs of young people and allow for the development and maintenance of existing relationships.

This precise pattern was unravelled by Mary (16) who had never succeeded at school, had truanted but not often, had left school at 15 with no income at all and clung to the future of 'dole' at 16. The removal of this allowance, the only hope she had, finally finished her home life, and five months before the interview she left home and lived for four weeks on the banks of the River Torrens. After losing a great deal of weight and in a depressed state she was taken in by friends; five months later she took an overdose and cut her wrists:

> I tried to O/D once because I couldn't hack it no more. I wasn't getting no money, no food, there was nothing, no family, I was just shaking and everything — pulse was up and I was sweating and going dizzy and I tried to slash my wrists and I got marks on my wrist — I tried to cut my wrist before. It was three or four weeks ago, we had a party drinking beer and everything got to me because I was sort of drunk and I got a piece of glass and started cutting my wrists. [Why?] Oh, I don't know, no money still, no money, no family — nothing. It's hopeless all the time.

At times the 'event' of breaking and entering served both the purpose of providing an income and of structuring the day. Like the fullness and richness of radio cricket commentaries the descriptions of breaking-in were vivid and precise.

> One time I was with one of my girlfriends. We went to this meeting at the shops and no-one had any money whatsoever and this girl who was there, she was really trying to get into the group, sort of thing, and she was saying we could all trust her, and she said she'd left the windows open. There was a guard dog there but because it was her house she went round and got the dog, an' that, and there was about five guys and two of us girls — I stood at the letterbox and was watching, and that, pretending I was waiting for someone, and she went round and opened the window and they cut the wire and they just forced it open, and I remember hearing this scream go bang! crash! and she goes 'Oh there goes my ornament, gone' — or something like that — Um, no lights were turned on and she led them through to where there was this, like a jewelry box or something — some sort of box where this money was kept — they

were going away on holiday and they'd saved it all up. We only took
50 — we only took 50 cause we were scared that if we did get caught
it would be worse.

In all cases they came to regard stealing as a disease: something they had to
be cured of, something that they were battling against in a brave effort to
accept their poverty, to accept the bottom of the pile, as they began the painful
process of learning to be poor.

I don't do it no more — I can handle being without money — I can
handle it now. If I'm broke I just come here — I don't steal no more.

I got done for smashing windows at school — four months ago it
was, it was over at the North Primary school. I was looking for my
lighter cause I dropped it — night time — the cops came over, and
my friend smiles a bit and the copper says 'Smack!' knocks him to
the ground and he goes 'Don't laught at me'. I'm all right now, my
soccer coach is a policeman. If I've got no money I just stays at
home.

Never in the six weeks which I spent with them did any of these young
people suggest that they might return to school. Several had tried to go back,
and failed once more. Several had finished CYSS schemes and further education
courses, and they had all acquired skills which, although unmarketable, they
clung to as examples of their individuality, their creativity, their humanity.

I've got a thing about Egyptology — I've written masses about it
and I'm always reading about it. I've got no maths though. I need an
education: so I'd like to go back, but then I couldn't keep up with it
unless I did year 8 and year 9 all over again, but I don't think I could
do it — I could do Egyptology — I went for a job in the museum in
the Egyptology department but I didn't get it.

I was thinking of, about doing industrial sewing cause I'm a good
sewer — I make skirts an' that for me sister.

My sister designs clothes — she's got a whole book that thick of
clothes designs — she's going to do a fashion parade and I'm going
to be a model. They say I've got the right face for it.

I've got no talent, an' that. I've just got skills and sports, but no talent. My Mum's got no talent either, she's 40 years old and still plays netball.

I put my name at the CES and I done a CYSS course — Retail Sales — I went for an interview at John Martins but it didn't go too good cause it was my first interview. She said I got good eye contact — next time just try a bit harder and don't be so nervous, cause I was stumbling over my words, an' that.

As their high expectations for their new independence and their hopes for a life of work and social activities recede into the poverty of unemployment, so new ways of filling the day with normal activities become important. The loss of the regulated work day with its richness of social life and social rhythms drives most young unemployed people to extremes in their quest for an income, or what an income might buy. A workless life means a loss of working-class life, pushing young people into the unknown world of marginal labor, where they are exposed to exploitation and personal danger.

I went for a couple of jobs as a waitress. Fake name, fake age. Then I thought . . . the peek-a-boo girls (peep-show) an' that, and I thought I should, shouldn't I. It'll be extra money, anybody can do that sort of thing — but I didn't end up doing it — I got an interview and said I was 25 — I got to Adelaide but I chickened out.

This guy I was seeing had an older brother who was 35 and was setting up an escort agency and he was going to get me a car an' that — I would have done that cause I knew he would treat me right. At the time I was really desperate — I would only have had to do it two or three times a day.

When I was on the run I slept with guys but I wasn't getting paid. The guys were protecting me a lot — you know — they really protected me heaps.

Young Women and the Cash Economy

Young unemployed women were more susceptible to working in the cash economy than young men, being driven to accept both illegal conditions and illegal work. Even the most respectable businesses were found to have accounting practices that dealt frequently with only cash transactions. One young woman, after completing a TAFE beautician's course, got work at a nail-sculpting salon, only to find that she was paid in cash — no pay-slip, no tax, no questions asked. When she and her friend asked for a proper pay-slip they quickly found themselves on the dole and again back into training on a CYSS course. Another young woman worked for six months at a baker's shop and only demanded a pay-slip when the family realized something was wrong. She found herself quickly joining the unemployed statistics! During this study I encountered a range of jobs which were part of the cash economy including: waitressing, swimming lessons, nursing, tennis coaching, telephone selling and child care centre work, and I found that market places were used often for cash earnings; but the most institutionalized method of all was the 'vice' industry. The extent that young women work in the general area of 'vice', i.e., photographic studios, stripping, peek-a-boo, prostitution, is difficult to ascertain, but there is a generalized feeling from the police, bureaucrats, street-workers, and young women themselves, that this is an area of work that has increased in the last two years and is still expanding.

In a recent report in South Australia, the head of the Children's Interest Bureau stated: 'Young prostitutes often have . . . petty criminal records for offences other than prostitution, usually committed in order to survive. They are runaways and have low educational achievement and are often unemployed.' She went on to report that the 'federal government's decision to cease dole payments to 16–17-year-olds will further disadvantage an already alienated group.'

In the Victorian 'Inquiry into Prostitution', it was estimated by the police that there were 180 young people involved in prostitution in the state, whilst Hancock's research for the same inquiry showed 67 per cent of a sample of sixty-three young women had left school, and 85 per cent of those were unemployed; and the Fitzgerald inquiry in Queensland has been told of a 16-year-old who worked at 'Fantasy Photographic' agency during her school holidays, earning up to $1,800 a week.

The recent debate in South Australia has been around whether organized under-age prostitution exists. With the exception of reports of two such establishments, one in Port Adelaide and one at Dry Creek, there is little evidence of any organized approach. However, there is no doubt that young women, rather than under-aged women, are more desired by 'businesses', their services cost more, and they are in greater demand by clients, with some establishments specializing in young women, as against under-age women. It is doubtful whether the nicety of a legally defined age bracket has any effect on young women's responses. The fact that they have reached the age of 18 doesn't mean they feel less exploited, less helpless, less vulnerable; or for that matter more able, all of a sudden, to cope. By concentrating only on the legally under-aged a great deal remains unrecognized, invisible and unconcerning.

The 1986 'prostitutes of South Australia' phone-in of 108 calls showed that 54 per cent were under 21 when they started working, whilst the Victorian report showed only 34 per cent under 20, from a sample of ninety. However, workers were now working longer, with 54 per cent working two years or more, whilst in 1979 only 22 per cent worked longer than two years.

In the last year, there has been an explosion of escort agencies in Adelaide with 112 agencies now in existence and twenty-two brothels. The South Australian vice squad estimates around one hundred 18–20-year-olds to be working in the business and there seems little doubt that ages are getting lower, and harder to detect, and that prostitution, like war, is something experienced by the young: both young men and young women.

> My wage was only 40 odd dollars — I didn't know anybody (having just runaway to Melbourne). I started to go out. I started meeting people and I think it was in a pub in Coburg, and some old guy came over and offered me some money, and I said no. The next night there was this young guy, so I took it and that's how I started — it wasn't organized or anything — I wish I'd done it properly — it was the company I liked.

> I didn't care about the morals of it, I think I was too young — I was only 15. It was $20 then — now I think they got a bargain — a 15-year-old for $20. I was drinking an' that — it just seemd to happen.

By the age of 15 Jane had run away to Melbourne; she married at 16, became pregnant, lost her child, went to Perth; started to work as a stripper before being tempted by the money available in escort agencies.

The other young women Jane worked with had the following histories that connected them, inevitably, with the young women I had interviewed in Elizabeth.

(a) Left school 2nd year high. Almost illiterate.

    (b) Worked Hindley Street [red light district of Adelaide] at 14 — little schooling [described as no schooling].

    (c) Just started working. Left school at 15, worked in a supermarket six days a week for $180 — lived in a flat and started to shoplift.

    (d) Left school at 15. Ran away from home at 14 — slept around in exchange for housing. Became pregnant — stayed in single mothers' home. State housing emergency list — slept in park with baby. Now working to buy a home.

For these young women there is a sense of 'belonging' — bringing to them the normality of a working life that they have never had before.

> Even now some of the girls don't like the work but they like being part of something. The girls who work together get quite friendly — they like to belong.

And Sue, in Elizabeth, who had flirted with the idea of joining an escort agency herself, got the same feeling of 'belonging' from the drop-in centre that now held her life together.

> Do you ever watch *Cheers*? — the song in that is magic, it goes — 'Sometimes you need to go where everybody knows your name'. I walk into this place and feel welcome — we all know each other and we all care about each other, we muck around and we — you know — have a laugh and do really weird things . . . we all belong.

For many young women living on the street, that sense of 'belonging' is something that still eludes them. At the age of 16, having been 'provided' for by education policies, income policies, employment policies, training policies, control policies, they appear confused, abused and broken. Their 'talk' about themselves is a measurement not, as they see it, of their own failure, but the failure of policy, policy makers and Government.

Cathy   I hate me . . . Others hate me . . . People say things to me just to be nice and underneath, they're thinking I'm stupid. People only like me when they want something.

Marie   No one will believe me . . . It was my fault . . . I deserve to be punished . . . I'm dirty.

Diane   I'm stupid . . . I'm really crazy . . . It's all my fault, I should have looked after my mum, so she wouldn't resent me . . . sort of thing.

Vanessa   I'm not a person. Because mum didn't think I 'was there' (I was just there to do things for her) I thought I wasn't there . . . because I couldn't see anything . . . I didn't seem to know what was going on around me. I'm disgusting, dirty, a slut. I was called a fat slut by mum and my sisters . . . so I imagined myself cutting off hunks of flesh down to the bone . . . to get rid of myself. If I look at someone or they look at me . . . they will know how disgusting I am. Nobody wants to look at me and come near me unless they want to bash me up or . . . you know. I'm only around to do things for people and to let people do things to me. I thought that because I couldn't feel nothing. I was that close to becoming a prostitute in . . . but a voice inside me — which I could barely hear — stopped me.

Young People and the Law

The final and important plank of present Australian youth policies is that of increased regulation. Young people, now faced with unemployment, training, or part-time work, after eleven or twelve years in education, are creating new cultural responses that reflect the considerable change and crisis undergone by the Australian economy over the last three years. Central to this response is the question of space, its regulation and use, and the way that the new economic tensions felt by young people have brought into sharper focus the question of their visibility and the way that this is policed (Presdee, 1985, 1987, 1989, 1990a, 1990b).

The quest to find a space of your own, a place to gather, to do nothing, to spend one's unlimited free time, has taken on an even greater significance. Yet young people need a space in which to explore, to create an identity which is separate from the roles and expectations imposed by family, school and work.

Young people have become more visible in the wrong places, more of a problem, and as such greater attention is now being directed at developing ways to further regulate the 'free' space that young people currently occupy. If the issue of space and young people becomes more critical the answer will not lie in further policing, regulation and control but in a greater understanding of how and why young people use space and in allowing an element of autonomy and power that will enable young people to develop and be creative, to 'work it out'.

At a time when governments at both State and Federal level are intent — as in England — on deregulating the economic system, a countering force for increased social regulation has been released. It is only by enforcing control mechanisms that the unacceptable social side-effects of economic deregulation can be masked and portrayed as a moral, rather than an economic question. In this way the control of young people is separated from the question of employment. This is an inevitable consequence of attempting to put into place a youth policy that contains as its major thrust re-education programmes at a time of high unemployment. The response of governments to what is perceived as a crisis in law and order has been an undistinguished scramble to out-Rambo each other with promises of even tougher sentences, more regulations concerning the behaviour of young people in public spaces, shopping centres and on public transport, and promises of more and more policing. The culture of working-class unemployed youth is becoming, in effect, criminalized.

Those groups of young people that are faced with the further injustices of class, gender and race will particularly feel the inadequacies of youth policies that assume to know so much about the structure of their lives and their social practices. If the issue of 'space' is central to the experience of being young, and is the key area of concern in terms of daily playing out of contradictions, then the answer does not lie in imposing even further restrictions on the rights of young people and introducing even more regulations covering all aspects of their lives.

Conclusion

It has become clear that the identity of being 'a youth' is being transformed and reconstructed by youth policies both in Australia and elsewhere. This period of life is no longer transitory but is taking on a new meaning of its own that remains largely unexplored and unexplained. But it is also clear that youth policies that are aimed at constraining, constricting, and coercing young people along paths that lead nowhere, will be no substitute for policies that release young people into a troubled but adult social world.

'Priority One' was an attempt to introduce a range of policies —

education, training and social security — to help young Australians. In practice, by removing entitlement to wages and to adequate benefits, in an attempt to turn young people back to school or to training schemes, it can be shown to have significantly worsened their situation.

Policies that negate the world of the young will in the end create even more poverty and crime, marginalizing more young people than ever before.

Chapter 10

Youth Homelessness in Wales

Mark Liddiard and Susan Hutson

Within the past few years, and certainly since 1987 — 'The International Year of Shelter for the Homeless' — there has been an explosion of publicity surrounding youth homelessness in Great Britain, fuelled undoubtedly by a parallel expansion in the scale of the problem itself. Whilst this publicity has led to a greater awareness of the existence of youth homelessness and has certainly been of considerable benefit to those working in the field, media publicity has, by its very nature, been at times distorted and inappropriate. Moreover, much of this publicity has come from London, where the problem of youth homelessness is more visible, more accessible, and more explicit than elsewhere. Whilst such publicity is obviously welcomed, it has nevertheless led to the problem outside London being too often ignored.

This chapter, then, represents a move away from the large body of London-based material (Randall, 1988; O'Mahony, 1988) and is concerned, instead, with homeless young people in Wales. It will look at the numbers, the characteristics and the reasons behind youth homelessness there and it will consider how agencies are dealing with the problem on the ground. Youth homelessness, as an issue and as a day-to-day experience, cannot be considered apart from the fast changing backdrop of government policy and legislation.

The research is based on a research project carried out between May and October 1988 and funded by the West and Wales Region of The Children's Society, looking at 'street children' in Wales, by which was meant young people, under 18, living away from carers and without secure accommodation. The intention of the research was to assess the numbers and the characteristics of such young people and to evaluate current provision with a view to the establishment of a project in Wales. In accordance with our research brief, we conducted some eighty interviews with agencies involved, both statutory and voluntary, and twenty-three interviews with young people themselves in three major cities — Swansea, Cardiff and Newport — and in one rural county, Clwyd, in North Wales.

Although the initial interest of the funding body was young runaways, it soon became increasingly clear that the issue of 'homelessness' amongst young people presented a more extensive problem. 'Homelessness' is essentially a discretionary term and is defined in different ways, for different reasons. In this context, however, 'homelessness' is defined as: not being in, nor having immediate or easy access to secure accommodation.

Our research initially opened with a degree of doubt as to whether a youth homelessness problem even existed in Wales. At the most, it was expected that the problem would be fairly small in scale. However, the research proved this not to be the case. We discovered youth homelessness in Wales to be an increasingly significant issue — although one which is perhaps more concealed and less obvious than is the case in London.

The Numbers of Homeless

Certainly, estimating numbers is a notoriously unreliable way of assessing the extent of homelessness. Different estimates rely on different definitions of homelessness which can vary, on the one hand, from being literally 'roofless' through to simply living in an 'unsatisfactory housing situation' — be that sleeping rough, sleeping on a friend's floor or simply living in an unsuitable cohabiting situation. Furthermore, estimates tend to be based on those youngsters who are in contact with agencies. Yet it is obvious that the 'hidden majority' do not approach agencies for assistance for a variety of reasons. Some young people may believe that agencies have little or nothing to offer; whilst others may be homeless for such short periods of time — sleeping on a friend's floor for a few nights — that they may not, in fact, see themselves as being in need of any particular assistance. All these factors contribute to making any figures *ad hoc*, subjective and unreliable. Such figures tell us more about the nature of the agency collecting them than about homelessness itself.

However, we nevertheless asked the agencies we interviewed to estimate the number of homeless youg people under 18 that they had seen within the last year in order to gain an impressionistic idea of the problem. This gave us a total of 1,990. Whilst there was likely to be some overlap — the same client being mentioned by more than one agency — we must remember that not all agencies were visited; not all the agencies were able to give us estimates; and that many young people never visit agencies. Thus, it is likely that this figure of nearly 2,000 seriously understates the problem.

This figure must be seen against the statistics of two unpublished Welsh surveys of people presenting themselves as homeless in one month in 1985. In the survey by The West Glamorgan Homelessness Group, there were 168 such individuals of whom 68 per cent were between 16 and 25. In the survey by the Torfaen Committee for the Homeless, Gwent, in a more rural area, there were thirty-seven, of whom 52 per cent were 16–25. These figures are significant, even against the estimation from London (Randall, 1988) that, apart from the 1,700 young people who turn up at Centrepoint night-shelter every year, there are 50,000 more in temporary accommodation. These London figures break down into 1,000 in hostels; 1,800 in Bed and Breakfast; 900 in short-term housing; 2,000 in squats and 45,000 'in other households', which largely means sleeping on friends' floors.

Some Case Studies

In dealing with such large numbers, however, it is very easy to lose sight of the fact that behind statistical data lie the day-to-day lives and experiences of young people living without stable accommodation both in London and in the cities, towns and countryside of Wales. The following accounts give a clearer picture of their existence and predicament. Both of the examples used here were fortunate insofar as they eventually came into agency contact and were living in hostels.

Sharon

Sharon was 18 when we spoke to her. She had been living in a hostel for homeless young people for six months. A local girl, she had been in care since she was 13. As she said: 'It was children's homes into foster parents and foster parents into bed-sits'. In her first year out of care at $16\frac{1}{2}$, she had moved through six bed-sits. 'Normally the landlord's rent was too expensive or it was stinking — things like that'.

She told us: 'All the bed-sits I lived in, I don't think there was anybody over 20 in any of them — all about 16/17 . . . Quite a lot of them moved out from home — they just couldn't cope with the pressure. Some got kicked out. Some walked out.'

Sharon said that she would like somewhere of her own but, because she was living in a hostel, she could not be classed as 'priority homeless'. As she said: 'It's a bit of a Catch-22. Because you're living here, you're not classed as being homeless . . . They more or less tell you — if you haven't got a kid or are out on the streets, you've got no chance of getting a flat.'

Her experiences, although undramatic, were common to many of the youngsters we talked to: 'You go to the Citizen's Advice. They give you a list [of Bed and Breakfast addresses]. You go to the council. They give you a list. Then you walk around these places on the list and you might not find anywhere . . . People don't want to know . . . You go and sign on and they won't send you any money for about six to seven weeks. The landlord would be getting funny and you'd have to go down to the DHSS: "Oh, it's in the post". It was never in the post. You just had to keep going down and pushing them.'

Colin

Colin, although no longer under 18, had been living in a hostel for homeless young people for three months when we spoke to him. He had left home after arguments, particularly with his stepfather. He had rented a flat but was evicted when his landlord went abroad. His stepfather would not have him home and his gran could not help him. Colin told us that, consequently, he had lived in a tent for two-and-a-half months. His friend had brought him a flask each day. He had not known anyone else who had slept like that before.

Colin's problems did not stop when he was referred to the hostel by a policeman. He paints a dismal picture of hostel life: 'Cooking is really grotty . . . if you don't do your jobs someone else has to do them and you fall out then with other people . . . We have house meetings — how to cater for yourself and budgeting — but since some people have come in, it's just become complaints.'

Colin told us that he would like a place of his own but that he hasn't had any help in finding one.

Characteristics of the Homeless

Having established that there *are* large numbers of young people, under 18, who are homeless in Wales, what did the research tell us of their characteristics?

There is a traditional image of homelessness as affecting mostly middle-aged, white males. Although there is no reason why homeless young people should be predominantly white or male, it appears that these old stereotypes are often built into the agency responses.

The marked absence of ethnic minority groups from projects does not reflect the number of people from such groups who live in Wales, particularly Cardiff or Newport. An explanation that was given to us by agency workers was that ethnic minority communities 'look after their own'. Whilst this may be so, a more realistic explanation, if the London experience is correct, is that most agencies present an overwhelmingly white face — and this is even more true in Wales than in London. This white face deters many ethnic minority young people from using the facilities.

Similarly, whilst a few projects had a majority of female clients — usually a consequence of gender assumptions in the referral process — the majority were male-dominated, dealing with only a handful of women. This does not, however, mean that the problems which produce homelessness affect males more. It appears that young women experience and encounter the same family pressures and stresses as their male counterparts. In fact, at an earlier age (under 16) more young women run from home than young men and this fact has been connected with a higher incidence of sexual abuse amongst young women (Newman, 1989). Indeed, it was even suggested to us by an agency worker that because of the traditional stereotype associating women with the home, equivalent in some ways to the male association with employment, young women may in fact be worse affected by homelessness.

On occasions, it is true that young women can have better access to local authority housing than their male counterparts — particularly if they are pregnant. Moreover, agency workers speculated both that parents are more reluctant to turn out young women than young men and that young women will tolerate an unsatisfactory home situation for longer. However, a more frequently given explanation as to why fewer young women present themselves as homeless was that some young women who find themselves in a homeless situation may quickly acquire a partner and enter into a relationship which they might not otherwise have contemplated. As an agency worker told us: 'Very often, women tend to improvise . . . They end up staying with a boyfriend who they really *don't* want to be with, but they stay there because there's nowhere else to go.'

If homelessness amongst young women and young people from ethnic minority groups tends to be hidden, then it must be remembered that homelessness amongst young people *in general* also tends to be hidden. This hidden nature of homelessness is a practical and a methodological issue. It underscores every estimation of, or statement about, the problem.

In the case of homeless young people in Wales, there appeared to be remarkably little sleeping rough or even squatting. Even those agencies who claimed to have good information networks amongst homeless youngsters felt there were very few actually on the streets and, of the small number of those who *did* sleep rough, it was a predominantly short-term affair precipitated by a crisis. As James, a 17-year-old from Cardiff, told us: 'It's only a few people, a couple of days at a time 'til they can find somewhere else to live.' This reflects the London findings that youngsters generally seemed to sleep on friends' floors. Such young people are not easy to see or count. As an agency worker told us: 'They're sleeping on friends' floors — they don't exist; they don't appear on any register . . . '

If the ultimate solution to youth homelessness rests on access to suitable accommodation and on a situation where most low-rent accommodation is provided by the local authority, then the question of the mobility of young homeless people is important, especially since we found, throughout Wales, an understandable unwillingness of local authorities to house people who had come in from outside the area.

The findings of the Welsh research were that, although homeless youngsters appeared to be highly mobile, moving frequently within different types of insecure accommodation, this mobility generally occurred within the confines of their home town or, at most, their home county. It was clear that young people normally become homeless *initially* in their home area. This is not surprising as the minimal resource these young people have is local knowledge and contacts. It is usually only when local resources dry up that a young person may move further afield. This finding has clear implications for policy.

We did have some evidence, however, that those over 18 without secure accommodation, were more likely to move between towns and counties than the younger 16–18 age group the research was aimed at. However, very often, this mobility was forced on them by the Board and Lodging Regulations (discussed later).

Throughout the Welsh research we were very aware of distinctions between rural and urban areas. In much the same way as there have long been doubts over the extent of the problem in the provinces as opposed to London, so there has been equal doubt over the existence of rural, as opposed to urban, homelessness. However, it quickly became clear to us that rural areas did not differ in any significant way from urban areas in the incidence and characteristics of homelessness. In both the countryside and the town old cars, tents and the beach were used for sleeping rough. The processes creating homelessness in rural areas appear to be the same. If anything young people in rural areas can face greater problems in terms of accommodation and jobs than their urban contemporaries. Moreover there was noticeably less local agency support in the country than in the major cities. For example, in the rural *county* of Clwyd there were three agencies working directly with homeless youngsters, whilst in the *city* of Cardiff there were ten. A clear need was expressed for more facilities in rural areas. As one agency worker told us: 'The pressure of problems is less; but the availability of resources is less.'

In rural areas, for example, there tend to be few agencies to refer particular problems to, and the isolation of both the agency and the client can raise difficulties. The importance of *local* provision is particularly important in terms of accommodation. Whereas young people are willing and able to travel for advice, the majority want and need accommodation within their own local area.

In terms of the characteristics and needs of young homeless people, in Wales as elsewhere, probably the most essential thing to consider throughout is that they do not constitute an homogeneous group. One important difference will be that some will simply have housing problems, whilst others will face additional serious and severe problems, which may well have been compounded or intensified by the experience of homelessness. This variety and the way in which agencies classify their clients as 'ordinary', 'vulnerable' and 'very vulnerable' is an interesting problem in itself, but outside the scope of this paper. It is noted, though, that agencies tend to cater for the middle group, with which this paper is also largely concerned.

Presenting Reasons and Background Problems of Homeless Clients

What, then, are the reasons for homelessness? And why are these young people in the position in which they find themselves?

Clearly, such situations are fundamentally complex and rarely mono-causal. The whole 'cause and effect' issue is both difficult to pinpoint and even harder to quantify and, in the end, depends on whose perceptions are being considered. An agency's perception, for instance, may well view a client's homelessness as the result of rejection from the family, whereas the youngster may explain it in practical terms, as having nowhere suitable to live.

However, young people and agency workers were agreed on one point — that the most common reason for leaving, or being evicted from home, was family arguments. Over 50 per cent of the young people we spoke to mentioned family problems in relation to homelessness, and this finding is supported by two unpublished Welsh surveys where 'domestic disputes' was given as the reason for leaving the 'last settled base' by 73 per cent of the respondents in the survey in Torfaen, Gwent and 59 per cent of the respondents in the study in West Glamorgan. This response is, perhaps, not surprising when the current interpretation of many social problems is family centred. This interpretation suits both governments and often professionals, many of whom have been trained in basic psychology and counselling skills.

Yet it is important to be aware that there is a distinction between the 'background' and the 'presenting' problem. The 'presenting' problem may very well be the arguments, petty crime or partner issues culminating in an exit from home. The 'background' to such issues is of two main types: either deeper family/parental issues — be that sex abuse, physical abuse or reconstituted families — or on the other hand, the impersonal forces of the labour and housing markets combined with legislation in Britain today. Such differences in perception are highlighted by one agency worker, contrasting her own explanations with those of her young clients:

> It's whose perception really, isn't it? . . . It's either rejection from the family or anger at the care system, that's my perception . . . Their perception is much more practically based — there aren't any proper jobs for them; they haven't got anywhere to live that's suitable.

Past research has indicated that a large proportion of the young homeless in London have a care background (Department of Environment, 1981; Randall, 1988), suggesting that between 20–35 per cent of such youngsters have lived in care at some time — even though youngsters from care represent only 1 per cent of the population. The Welsh research supports such findings and would, if anything, push the figure higher.

Whilst the relationship between care and homelessness clearly requires close investigation, it is obvious that many young people who leave care at 16 or 17 often have no home base they can call their own. Many lack not only the accommodation a family can give, but also the support, financial and otherwise, which is so often given to young people by their parents and which is so important in a situation of unemployment (Hutson and Jenkins, 1989). As a consequence of lacking such initial resources youngsters from care are more likely to be subsequently at risk of homelessness than their counterparts at home.

The Risks of Homelessness

It is generally agreed that young homeless people under 18 in Wales are 'at risk'. However, there is significant disagreement over precisely what they are 'at risk' from. Traditionally, emphasis has been placed on drugs and prostitution. Whilst these are clearly important, there is a danger in overplaying such issues at the cost of understating, and even ignoring, other crucial factors.

Drugs, certainly, were felt by some workers to be part of the culture of some homeless youngsters living an unsettled way of life. They felt that young people often used drugs to cope with the inevitable hardships of everyday life. There is, however, an important distinction between drug *use* and drug *abuse*. Whilst the majority of the young people agencies dealt with had *used* drugs at some time or another, drug *abuse* did not appear to be a serious problem. This finding is clearly influenced, however, by the fact that we were dealing with young people under 18 and who were in touch with agencies. Alcohol abuse, on the other hand, was seen to be a particularly serious problem. As one drug agency worker said: 'Alcohol's not our brief... but don't get me wrong. I think alcohol is very high risk.' It appears that alcohol abuse tends to be underplayed whilst drug abuse is perhaps exaggerated — possibly because alcohol use is part of the social fabric in a way that drug abuse is not.

Similarly, whilst prostitution is commonly perceived as one of the biggest risks of street life for both girls and boys, and features predominantly in media accounts, in Wales there was little evidence of structured prostitution — although, again, this may well reflect the fact that the youngsters we spoke to, or heard about, were those who were in touch with agencies. We were told by agency workers that a number of women *did*, however, exchange sexual favours for shelter and food. One agency worker told us of a 15-year-old girl, who had left school with the permission of both her headmaster and her parents and was living in a flat with no money to pay the rent. The agency worker felt: 'There was a definite feeling that the landlord was allowing her to stay there because, at some point, he was going to ask her to do something for him. It could have been anything, couldn't it?'

However, we suggest (Hutson and Liddiard, 1989) that more general offending — including theft and 'survival' offending — is the main risk for young people living away from a stable base in Wales. As James told us:

> In my experience, most of them kip down [sleep rough] for less than two weeks — that's usually when they turn to burglaries, simply for food. I came close to it when I was sleeping rough. With three days and no food, you get desperate.

Yet in saying this, we would not like to minimize the importance of prostitution and drug abuse. We would like to highlight two other dangers. Health care provision is minimal and difficult to obtain for such young homeless people in unstable accommodation. Access to mainstream health services seemed to depend more on the concern of the individual GP rather than on a recognized structure of provision appropriate to young people. Moreover, several agency workers felt that the worst consequences of homelessness were the less tangible effects that such an experience can have on motivation and self respect and the resultant alienation from mainstream adult life.

Statutory and Voluntary Agencies

The situation is made more problematic by the fact that the provision of services to young homeless people between 16 and 25 is complicated by a variety of laws which change as a young person gradually moves into adult status. This complexity is compounded by the fact that both statutory and voluntary agencies work in this area. They work within certain legal responsibilities and within the limits of their funding.

In terms of statutory involvement, both Social Services and the Housing Department are the main providers of services to homeless young people. Social Services are responsible for young people until they leave care, normally at 17 (but at 19 if they come into care at 16 or over). In addition they can 'advise and befriend' young people up to 21. Thus Social Services' policies are vitally important, especially for the large number of homeless youngsters with a care background. Moreover, it was often felt that under-18s in general were the responsibility of Social Services and this is legally the case with all those under 16. However, in practice, as one agency worker told us: 'By the time they're 15 or 16, it's very difficult to get Social Services to take on a new case.'

At the same time, however, many other services, such as the Housing Department, effectively do not begin to take responsibility for youngsters until they are 18 or over. Consequently, there is a very real and crucial gap in provisions for this intermediate group of 16–18-year-olds. As James (17) told us:

So I was stuck, sort of, in the middle — I was either too young or too old. The Social Services stop at 16 and then the other services start when you're 18, so most of us people seem to be 17...

There is, in fact, an implicit assumption within such services that most youngsters under 18 will remain living at home.

All the Social Service Departments we spoke to have some type of 'leaving care' policy or scheme. These ranged from a continuation in 'family placement' in one county; to the 'topping up' of benefits for young people in care in another; whilst, in one city, 16–18-year-olds were offered a mixture of residential care, hostels or Bed and Breakfast lodgings with social work support. Clearly, the evaluation, continuation and possible extension of such schemes is vital if the vastly disproportionate number of homeless youngsters leaving care is ever going to be dealt with.

It is frustrating, in view of this, that any moves to extend the involvement of the Social Services with young people up to 21 years runs hard against the 'alternative to care' policies being pursued within many Departments and which can be seen as part of the wider movement of care into the community.

The responsibilities of the Housing Department are set out in the 1977 Housing Homeless Persons Act and the 1985 Housing Act. These Acts effectively define someone as homeless if they, together with anyone normally resident with them, have no accommodation which they are entitled to occupy, or cannot secure entry into such accommodation. The main problems that arise concern the criteria which finally determine whether or not someone qualifies for assistance. Not only must a person have a local connection of some sort — providing evident problems under Board and Lodgings regulations — but a person must also *not* be '*intentionally* homeless'. This effectively rules out anyone walking out from a parental home or from a partner where violence cannot be proved. In addition to these strict criteria, a person must show that they are in a 'priority need' or a 'vulnerable' category. Whilst 'priority need' can be related to old age, mental illness, handicap or pregnancy, the Acts do *not* class youngsters under 18 as specifically vulnerable, simply by virtue of their age. Consequently, 'vulnerability' is clearly open to interpretation by the housing officer. The following quotation, although somewhat humorous, shows well the force of interpretation and stereotyping which inevitably occurs:

> There are people I won't declare as vulnerable — for example a bully like the ones probation sent down. They're just yobos. I feel these people shouldn't have special treatment. Big muscles and vests. They are not vulnerable. *We* are vulnerable. They are burglars, all sorts.

It is clear that the crux of youth homelessness in Wales, as elsewhere, lies in the availability of suitable accommodation and a reasonable income to obtain it. It is also clear that public sector housing is under pressure due to financial restrictions and uncertainty over the future of public housing in Britain. It is obvious that as increasing financial constraints are placed on Local Authorities, so growing numbers of homeless young people will be classed as ineligible under the Acts. The selling-off of council stock, the long term shrinkage of the private rented sector and the current emphasis on private home ownership all make the housing situation of these young people increasingly problematical.

Whatever provision may be set up for young homeless people, the whole notion of emergency provision soon collapses if subsequent move-on accommodation is unavailable. Many of the hostels, day centres and emergency accommodation projects are provided by the voluntary sector in Wales, as in other parts of Britain. Some of these agencies, such as the Cyrenians and The

Salvation Army, have extended their concern to cover the increasing numbers of young people, whilst agencies specializing in the young homeless such as Shelter and the Young Single Homeless Group are already experts in the field. Other agencies, like Barnardos and The Children's Society, are moving into this new field with the closing down of their residential care establishments. In some cases voluntary agencies are working in partnership with Social Services. As we have already mentioned, many agencies tend to cater for specific categories of young people and we have already discussed the way in which homelessness amongst women and ethnic minorities tends to remain hidden. Other agencies feel it necessary to target the more traditional homeless groups — particularly when funds are available through the national restructuring of the Resettlement Units which catered primarily for vagrants:

> Because there's a traditional, white, middle-aged male idea of what homelessness is, many projects still target their resources at these traditional groups. They are highly visible . . . The police don't like them living on the streets. The City Council don't like them living on the streets. So, consequently, anyone that does anything, will get handouts.

In addition, accommodation agencies tend not to cater for what they call 'high risk' clients partly because few have twenty-four hour cover. Moreover, such clients, whether their 'risk' stems from disability or anti-social behaviour, can be disruptive, put at risk the good name of the project or stigmatize more 'normal' clients. These 'high risk' clients are often referred to specialist agencies, such as for example drug agencies or — in the last resort — prison or psychiatric hospital.

Fundamentally, then, agencies can often only take a *curative* as opposed to a *preventative* approach — dealing only with the symptoms of the problem rather than the causes — largely because many agencies in Wales are operating, very much, on a hand-to-mouth basis such that they can: ' . . . do no more than jump from one crisis to another'. Whilst a few projects *did* attempt preventative work — predominantly in the form of education — large numbers of agencies considered such preventative work valuable, yet financially unrealistic. The statutory agencies — Education, the Youth Service, the Careers Service — played very little part here. It would appear that their brief is to deal with essentially 'non-problematic' young people. Moreover, we were told that agencies, with statutory responsibilities, are often loath to admit a problem before they have a solution.

However, one important part of the work that some agencies, for example Shelter Wales, *can* do for young homeless people is that of exerting political pressure. Whilst there is much debate over the relative merits and benefits of such political pressure, it nevertheless does seem, on occasions, to have changed, or at least influenced, relevant policy and decision-making.

Agency cooperation and coordination is an important and interesting issue and it was clear, in the Welsh research, that rivalries between agencies, which were often long standing and quite unconnected with the problem of homelessness, sometimes hindered work on the ground. As one agency worker said: 'There's all these issues that have separated these agencies over a long period and you've got to plough through those to try and find common ground.'

Some workers told us of the disadvantages of cooperation — the delays which are often part of a democratic process and the loss of independence often necessary for experimentation. However, despite the accusations that agencies were 'more concerned with treading on one another's toes than treating something in a community context' and that voluntary agencies were being used, at best, as subcontractors and at worst, as 'dumping grounds', there was a growing awareness of the potential advantages of improved cooperation and coordination. There was, after all, a feeling that they all faced the same problems. As one agency worker said: 'We can slag them off. They can slag us off. But we're all suffering from the same problem — it's just lack of money and resources.'

Legislation and Young Homeless People

Dissatisfaction was expressed time and time again with the wider political and economic structures within which agencies have to work on both a short and a long term basis. Such structures are, essentially, set up by Government policy and legislation. It was in this area, above all, that there was constant criticism from both agency workers and young people themselves. It would seem that much of the legislation, formed against a broad political and economic backdrop, ignores the day-to-day experiences of youngsters who, for whatever reason, find themselves homeless.

Legislation in this area is complex, confusing and rapidly changing. Much of it was felt to be inappropriate and contradictory. As one particularly astute informant said: 'Law is an imprecise way of dealing with human relationships'.

The legislation affecting youth homelessness is manifold and varied. There are laws dealing specifically with homelessness, such as the Housing (Homeless Persons) Act 1977 and the Housing Act 1985. There is legislation affecting benefits, such as Income Support and Housing Benefit, and legislation concerning YTS and the Poll Tax, all of which will affect young homeless people in the future.

Having already discussed the 1977 and the 1985 Housing Acts in general terms, probably the most heavily criticized legislation in this area was the 1985 Board and Lodging Regulations which, although specifically dealing with over-18s, are nevertheless fundamental for youth homelessness in general. Under these regulations, certain claimants under 26 could only claim rent for Bed and Breakfast hotels for short periods of time — varying from eight weeks in Greater London, Birmingham, Manchester and Glasgow to just two weeks in coastal areas and four weeks elsewhere. When this time period expired, they had to leave the area and not return to claim benefit for six months in order to obtain the full board and lodging benefit again. Clearly, the expectation of finding both accommodation and employment in a period as short as just two weeks was quite unrealistic.

The recent 1988 changes in the DSS and the Housing Benefits are proving even more fundamental in their effect. As a consequence of these profound changes, not only are benefit levels related to *age*, as opposed to *need*, but Income Support is paid in arrears, so that youngsters have to wait two weeks before they receive Income Support and even longer for Housing Benefit. This has subsequently destroyed the unsatisfactory, yet nevertheless frequently used, option of Bed and Breakfast accommodation which requires money in advance, both in terms of rent and a deposit. This is having a profound effect on many emergency projects which have used Bed and Breakfast accommodation extensively, yet with clear reservations, for moving people on. Now this option is closed, projects are increasingly faced with the dilemma of either putting youngsters back out on the streets or allowing their own emergency accommodation to get silted up with people who have nowhere else to move on to.

Similarly, problems have been created by the replacement of the old system of single payments for one-off items such as furniture or a deposit for rent in advance, by loans from the Social Fund. Moreover, these loans must be paid back out of benefit. Furthermore, in their selection procedure for these loans, low priority is given to young people and to payment of rent in advance, whilst no loans are available for deposits in order to secure accommodation. Consequently, even those youngsters lucky enough to find themselves accommodation are often unable to take up the tenancy.

At the same time, in 1988, there were significant changes to the Housing Benefit system, the major change being that, whilst people can still receive 100 per cent of their rent and 80 per cent of general rates, claimants, even those on maximum Housing Benefit, must still pay at least 20 per cent of their general rates charge and all their water rates. This puts an additional financial pressure on young tenants, already economically weak and marginalized.

In addition to these changes in legislation, the removal of entitlement to Income Support from most 16- and 17-year-olds in September 1988, is already having serious consequences. Young people under 18 are now expected to find either a job or a YTS scheme. Consequently, 16- and 17-year-olds who have left school and who are unable to find work, and — for whatever reason — do not or cannot join a YTS scheme, are effectively without any independent income. Whilst there *are* certain exemption categories, young homeless people are *not* included as such, despite the fact that homeless youngsters are, of necessity, less likely to be able to maintain their place on a YTS scheme than their more secure contemporaries. As we were told: 'If you're homeless, what you spend your day doing is trying to find somewhere to sleep that night . . . It's impossible to stay on a YTS scheme.'

Although effectively dealing with youngsters over 18, the Community Charge or Poll Tax is, nevertheless, likely to have far reaching consequences for young people, requiring all claimants, even those on maximum benefit, to meet 20 per cent of the charge. Moreover, the tax is likely to encourage a move away from home by young people because of the additional pressure of having to pay an extra charge for anyone over 18 living in their household placed on families often already under financial strain. As one agency worker said: 'If you're getting problems now, with parents on Housing Benefit having to pay a charge for a lad and he is told to leave — just put Poll Tax on top of it and what's it going to be like?' Additionally, friends and relatives are going to be far less likely to welcome young people into their homes to sleep on their floors — which is currently a major strategy for homeless youngsters.

Within the legislation, in general then, it would appear that inadequate thought and understanding have been given to the issues of young people and homelessness with the result that much legislation is often inadequate, inappropriate and sometimes contradictory. For instance, it is clear that the whole thrust of the recently introduced legislation is to keep young people under 25, and particularly those under 18, at home. Yet, this ignores youngsters who, for whatever reason, have no home or secure base to call their own. Paradoxically, such legislation is in stark contradiction to the Board and Lodging regulations, which necessarily forced young people to become highly mobile, and to the Poll Tax which is likely to encourage the expulsion of youngsters over 18 from the parental home.

The Future?

Clearly then, the situation for homeless youngsters is unlikely to improve without significant and quite drastic changes in policy concerning the access of these young people to housing, jobs and benefits. Although unemployment levels may be falling off in some parts of the country, the increase in Welsh jobs — hoped for as part of urban-based economic recovery — is unlikely to produce jobs suitable for these young people with few formal qualifications and little training. It is equally unlikely that the stock of suitable accommodation will increase and it is this availability of accommodation which determines, ultimately, the criteria by which Housing Departments will house young people. Lastly, any improvement in benefits would contradict the basic tenets of a Conservative Government. At the same time, 'special' measures for 'special' cases would go against the whole philosophy of 'care in the community' and the basic beliefs of many agencies working in the field.

It is clear, therefore, that the situation of young homeless people in Wales is unlikely to improve in the foreseeable future. Nor is it likely to develop into the situation found at present in London — partly because few young people are likely to be drawn into the cities of South Wales in search of work, and because of the differences in the two housing markets. However, having said this, the full implications of recently introduced legislation are still to be fully played out in Wales. There is, for example, evidence of a core group of homeless youngsters under 18 who, as a consequence of the YTS regulations, effectively have no legal income. Yet how the Poll Tax and other legislation are affecting the situation is less than clear. In conclusion, it would appear that the immediate future for the youth homelessness situation in Wales is a bleak one.

We will, however, end on an optimistic note, not in any way justified by our main findings, by giving the account of one young man in Swansea. We were told his story by a social worker:

> We had an 18-year-old. He left residential care. He went into a hostel. They wouldn't have him because of his style of living. He got drunk and he would fight . . . He came back into care. Then he left. We got him a *job*. We prepared him for independent living. We got him a council *flat*. The staff helped him with the DHSS and got him furniture together. He came in from an identifiably homeless setting and then moved into independent living. He's still there.

This account involves cooperation on a local level between statutory and voluntary services against a background of benefit considerably more generous in 1987 than it is today. In this account the words *flat* and *job* indicate that, without these necessary props of adult life, few of the 2,000 youngsters we heard about in Wales will be able to leave the homeless scene, become independent, self supporting and return to mainstream life.

References

ABBOTT, P. and WALLACE, C. (1989) 'The Family', in Brown, P. and Sparks, R. (Eds) *Beyond Thatcherism*, Milton Keynes, Open University Press.

AINLEY, P. (1988) *From School to YTS: Education and Training in England and Wales 1944–1987*, Milton Keynes, Open University Press.

AINLEY, P. and CORNEY, M. (1990) *Training for the Future: The Rise and Fall of the Manpower Services Commission*, London, Cassells.

ASHTON, D. N. and FIELD, D. (1976) *Young Workers*, London, Hutchinson.

ASHTON, D. N., MAGUIRE, M. J. and GARLAND, V. (1982) *Youth in the Labour Market*, Research Paper No. 34, London, Department of Employment.

ASHTON, D. N. and MAGUIRE, M. J. (1986) *Young Adults in the Labour Market*, Research Paper No. 55, London, Department of Employment.

ASHTON, D. N., MAGUIRE, M. J. and SPILSBURY, M. (1990) *Restructuring thr Labour Market: the Implications for Youth*, Basingstoke, Macmillan.

ATKINSON, P. and REES, T. L. (Eds) (1982) *Youth Unemployment and State Intervention*, London, Routledge and Kegan Paul.

AUSTRALIAN BUREAU OF STATISTICS (1988) Catalogue 6203.0 Table 11, March 1988.

BADDELY, S. (1985) 'Criteria for Approved Training Organizations', *Youth Training News* No. 25, Manpower Services Commission, Sheffield.

BANKS, M. H. and ULLAH, P. (1988) *Youth Unemployment in the 1980s: Its Psychological Effects*, London, Croom Helm.

BARTON, L. and WALKER, S. (Eds) (1984) *Social Crisis and Educational Research*, London, Croom Helm.

BATES, I., CLARK, J., COHEN, P., MOORE, R. and WILLIS, P. (1984) *Schooling for the Dole*, London, Macmillan.

BEDEMAN, T. and COURTENAY, G. (1982) *One in Three: The Second National Survey of Young People on YOP*, Research and Development Series, No. 3, Sheffield, Manpower Services Commission.

BELL, C., HOWIESON, C., KING, K. and RAFFE, D. (1988) *Liaisons Dangereuses? Education-Industry Relationships in the first Scottish TVEI Pilot Projects*, Sheffield, Training Agency.

BENN, C. and FAIRLEY, J. (Eds) (1985) *Challenging the MSC*, London, Pluto Press.

BLACK, P. (1988) *National Curriculum: Task Group Report on Assessment*, London, Department of Education and Science.

BLAND, R. (1979) 'Measuring Social Class', *Sociology*, 13(2), pp. 283–91.

BOOTHBY, J., TUNGATT, M. TOWNSEND, A. R. and COLLINS, M. F. (1981) *A Sporting Chance?*, London, Sports Council Study 22.

BRAKE, M. (1980) *The Sociology of Youth and Youth Sub-Cultures*, London, Routledge & Kegan Paul.

BROOMHEAD, S. and COLES, B. (1988) 'Youth Unemployment and the growth of "New Further Education" ', in Coles, B. (Ed.) *Young Careers*, Milton Keynes, Open University Press.

BROWN, P. and ASHTON, D. N. (Eds) (1987) *Education, Unemployment and Labour Markets*, Basingstoke, Falmer Press.

BULMER, M. (1991) 'Successful Applications of Sociology: Can Britain Learn from Abroad', in Payne, G. and Cross, M. *Sociology in Action*, London, Macmillan.

BURGHES, L. (1987) *Made in the USA: A Review of Workfare, the Compulsory Work for Benefits Regime*, London, Unemployment Unit.

BURNHILL, P. (1984) 'The Ragged Edge of Compulsory Schooling', in Raffe, D. *Fourteen to Eighteen*, Aberdeen, Aberdeen University Press.

BURTON, J. (1987) *Would Workfare Work? A Feasibility Study of a Workfare System to Replace Long Term Unemployment in the UK*, Buckingham, University of Buckingham.

BYNNER, J. and STRIBLEY, K. M. (Eds) (1978) *Social Research Principles and Procedures*, Milton Keynes, Open University Press.

BYNNER, J. (1987) 'Coping with transition: ESRC's new 16–19 initiative', *Youth and Policy*, **22**, pp. 25–8.

CASEY, B. (1986) 'The "Dual Apprenticeship" System and the Recruitment and Retention of Young Workers in West Germany', *British Journal of Industrial Relations*, **24**, 1, pp. 63–84.

CHANDLER, E. J. (1989) 'Youth Training and the Limits of Vocationalism', paper presented to the British Sociological Association Conference, Plymouth, April: mimeo, Plymouth Polytechnic.

CHANDLER, E. J. and WALLACE, C. (1990) 'Some Alternatives in Youth Training: Franchise and Corporatist Models Compared', in Gleeson, D. (Ed.) *Training and its Alternatives*, Milton Keynes, Open University Press.

CHAPMAN, P. G. and TOOZE, M. (1987) *The Youth Training Scheme in the United Kingdom*, Aldershot, Avebury.

CHISHOLM, L. and BROWN, P. (1990) *Childhood, Youth and Social Change*, Basingstoke, Falmer.

CLEVELAND COUNTY COUNCIL CAREERS SERVICE (1988) *Report of the Principal Careers Officer to Careers and Youth Employment Sub-Committee*, October.

CLEVELAND COUNTY COUNCIL CAREERS SERVICE (1989) *Report of the Principal Careers Officer to Careers and Youth Employment Sub-Committee*, March.

CLEVELAND COUNTY COUNCIL, RESEARCH AND DEVELOPMENT UNIT (1987) *Cleveland 1987–1991: An Economic, Demographic and Social Review*.

CLEVELAND COUNTY COUNCIL, RESEARCH AND DEVELOPMENT UNIT (1988) *Cleveland 1988–1992: An Economic, Demographic and Social Review*.

CLOUGH, E., GRAY, J., JONES, B. and PATTIE, C. (1988) *Routes Through YTS*, Research and Development No. 42, Youth Cohort Studies No. 2, Sheffield, Manpower Services Commission.

COCKBURN, C. (1987) *Two Track Training*, Basingstoke, Macmillan.

COFFIELD, F. (1984) 'Is there Work After the MSC?', *New Society*, pp. 29–30.

COHEN, S. (1972) *Folk Devils and Moral Panics*, London, Paladin.

COLE, M. (1984) 'Teaching Till Two Thousand: Teachers' Consciousness in Time of Crises', in Barton, L. and Walker, S. (Eds) *Social Crisis and Education Research*, London, Croom Helm.

COLEMAN, J. S. (1961) *The Adolescent Society*, New York, Glencoe Free Press.

COLES, B. (1986) 'School Leaver, Job Seeker, Dole Reaper: Young and Unemployed in Rural England', in Allen, S., *et al.* (Eds) *The Experience of Unemployment*, London, Macmillan.

COLES, B. (1988a) 'The Rise of Youth Unemployment and the Growth of New Vocationalism', in Coles, B. (Ed.) *Young Careers*, Milton Keynes, Open University Press.

COLES, B. (1988b) 'The Decline of Youth Unemployment and the Eclipse of New Vocationalism', in Coles, B. (Ed.) *Young Careers*, Milton Keynes, Open University Press.

COLES, B. (1988c) 'Post-16 "progression" in a rural shire county', in Coles, B. (Ed.) *Young Careers: the Search for Jobs and the New Vocationalism*, Milton Keynes, Open University Press, pp. 66–85.

CROSS, M. (1987a) 'Who goes where? Placement and black youth on YTS', in Cross, M. and Smith, D. (Eds) *Black Youth Futures*, National Youth Bureau, pp. 44–58.

CROSS, M. (1987b) ' "Equality of Opportunity" and inequality of outcome: the MSC, ethnic minorities and training policy', in Jenkins, R. and Solomos, J. (Eds) *Racism and Equal Opportunity Policies in the 1980s*, Cambridge, Cambridge University Press, pp. 73–92.

CROSS, M. (1988) 'Ethnic minority youth in a collapsing labour market: the UK experience', in Wilpert, C. (Ed.) *Entering the Working World: Following the Descendants of Europe's Immigrant Labour Force*, Aldershot, Gower, pp. 56–88.

CROSS, M., WRENCH, J. and BARNETT, S. (1990) *Ethnic Minorities and the Careers Service: an Investigation into Processes of Assessment and Placement*, Department of Employment Research Paper No. 73, London, HMSO.

DALE, R. (Ed.) (1985a) *Education, Training and Employment: Towards a New Vocationalism?*, Oxford, Pergamon Press.

DALE, R. (1985b) 'The background and inception of TVEI', in Dale, R. (Ed.) *Education, Training and Employment*, Milton Keynes, Open University Press, pp. 41–56.

DAVIES, B. (1986) *Threatening Youth: Towards a National Youth Policy*, Milton Keynes, Open University Press.

DEAKIN, B. M. and PRATTEN, C. F. (1987) 'Economic Effects of YTS', *Employment Gazette*, **95**, 1, pp. 491–497.

DEAN, J. P. and FOOTE WHYTE, W. (1978) 'How do you know if the informant is telling the truth?', in Brynner, J. and Stribley, K. M. (Eds) *'Social Research Principles and Procedures*, Milton Keynes, Open University Press.

DEEM, R. (1986) *All Work and No Play?*, Milton Keynes, Open University Press.

DEPARTMENT OF EDUCATION AND SCIENCE (1989) *Science in the National Curriculum*, London, HMSO.

DEPARTMENT OF EMPLOYMENT (1977) *Young People and Work*, London, HMSO.

DEPARTMENT OF EMPLOYMENT (1987) 'Education and Labour Market Status of Young People', *Employment Gazette*, **93**, 8.

DEPARTMENT OF EMPLOYMENT, TRAINING AGENCY (1989) *Enterprise in Higher Education: Key Features of the Enterprise in Higher Education Proposals 1988–89*, Sheffield, Moorfoot.

DEPARTMENT OF EMPLOYMENT (1988) *Employment for the 1990s* Cmnd 540, London, HMSO (White Paper).

DEPARTMENT OF ENVIRONMENT (1981) *Single and Homeless*, London, HMSO.

DODDS, S., FURLONG, A. and CROXFORD, L. (1989) 'Quality and quantity: reducing non-contract attrition in a longitudinal survey', *Sociology*, **23**, pp. 275–84.

DOMBOIS, R. (1989) 'Flexibility by Law? The West German Employment Promotion Act and Temporary Employment', *Cambridge Journal of Economics*, **13**, pp. 359–71.

DUNNELL, K. (1976) *Family Formation*, London, HMSO.

EDWARDS, T. (1984) *The Youth Training Scheme: A New Curriculum? Episode One*, Basingstoke, Falmer Press.

Employment Gazette (1985) 'Rule Changes in YTS', July.

FINEGOLD, D. and SOSKICE, F. (1988) 'The failure of training in Britain: analysis and prescriptions', *Oxford Review of Economic Policy*, **4**, pp. 21–53.

FINN, D. (1986a) 'YTS: The Jewel in the Crown of the MSC', in Benn, C. and Fairley, J. (Eds) *Challenging the MSC*, London, Pluto.

FINN, D. (1986b) 'Free Enterprise', *Unemployment Bulletin*, **22**, Winter.

FINN, D. (1987) *Training Without Jobs*, Basingstoke, Macmillan.

FOORD, J. *et al.* (1985) 'The Quiet Revolution: Social and Economic Change on Teesside 1965–1985', a Special Report for BBC Northeast.

FOORD, J. *et al.* (1986/87) 'Living with Economic Decline: Teesside in Crisis', in *Northern Economic Review*, Winter, **14**, pp. 33–48.

FURLONG, A. (1986) 'Schools and the Structure of Female Occupational Aspirations', *British Journal of Sociology of Education*, **7**, 4, pp. 367–77.

FURLONG, A. (1987a) *The Effects of Youth Unemployment on the Transition from School to Work.* Unpublished PhD thesis, University of Leicester.

FURLONG, A. (1987b) 'Coming to Terms with the Declining Demand for Youth Labour', in Brown, P. and Ashton, D. N. (Eds) *Education, Unemployment and Labour Markets*, Basingstoke, Falmer Press.

FURLONG, A. and RAFFE, D. (1989) *Young People's Routes into the Labour Market*, ESU Research Paper No. 17, Edinburgh, Industry Department for Scotland.

FURLONG, A. and SPEARMAN, M. (1989) 'Psychological well-being and the transition from school', *British Journal of Education and Work*, 3(1), pp. 49–55.

GARNER, C., MAIN, G. N. and RAFFE, D. (1988) 'The Tale of Four Cities', in Raffe, D. (Ed.) *Education and the Youth Labour Market*, Basingstoke, Falmer Press.

GIDDENS, A. (1976) *New Rules of Sociological Method*, London, Hutchinson.

GLEESON, D. (Ed.) (1987) *TVEI*, Milton Keynes, Open University Press.

GOFFMAN, E. (1968) *Asylums*, Harmondsworth, Penguin.

GREEN, A. 'Education and Training: Under New Masters', in Wolpe, A. and Donald, J. (Eds) *Is there Anyone Here from Education?*, London, Pluto.

GRIFFIN, C. (1985) *Typical Girls?*, London, Routledge.

Guardian (1989) 'Business Scheme's Failure Rate Alarms MPs', 9 March.

GURNEY, M. (1980) 'The effects of unemployment on the psycho-social development of school-leavers', *Occupational Psychology*, **53**, pp. 205–13.

HAKIM, C. (1979) *Occupational Segregation: a Comparative Study of the Degree and Pattern of the Differentiation Between Britain, the United States and Other Countries*, London, Department of Employment.

HALL, S. and JEFFERSON, T. (1977) *Resistance through Rituals*, London, Hutchinson.

HAMILTON, S. F. (1987) 'Work and maturity: occupational socialisation of non-college youth in the United States and W. Germany', in *Research in the Sociology of Education and Socialisation*, **7**, pp. 283–312.

HANTRAIS, L. and KAMPHORST, T. J. (Eds) (1987) *Trends in the Arts: A Multi-national Perspective*, Amersfoort, The Netherlands, Giordano Bruno.

HARGREAVES, D. (1967) *Social Relations in a Secondary School*, London, Routledge.

HEATH, A. (1981) *Social Mobility*, London, Fontana.

HEDGES, B. and WITHERSPOON, S. (1984) *YTS Providers' Survey*, London, Social and Community Planning Research.

HENDRY, L. B., RAYMOND, M. and STEWART, C. (1984) 'Unemployment, school and leisure: an adolescent study', *Leisure Studies*, **3**, pp. 175–87.

HERGET, H. (1986) *The Transition of Young People into Employment After Completion of Apprenticeship in the "Dual System"*, Findings from a Research Project of the Federal Institute of Vocational Training, Berlin, European Centre for the Development of Vocational Training (CEDEFOP).

HUGHES, J. M. (Ed.) (1984) *The Best Years*, Aberdeen, Aberdeen University Press.

HUNT, J. and SMALL, P. (1981) *Employing Young People: A Study of Employers' Attitudes, Policies and Practices*, Edinburgh, Scottish Council for Research in Education.

HUTSON, S. and JENKINS, R. (1989) *Taking the Strain. Families, Unemployment and the Transition to Adulthood*, Milton Keynes, Open University Press.

HUTSON, S. and LIDDIARD, M. (1989) *Street Children in Wales: A study of runaways and homeless young people in four Welsh counties*, Cardiff, Children's Society.

INDUSTRY DEPARTMENT FOR SCOTLAND (1988) *New Entrants to the Labour Market in the 1990s*, ESU Discussion Paper No. 19., Edinburgh, Industry Department for Scotland.

INSTITUTE FOR MANPOWER STUDIES (1984) *Competence and Competition*, London, MSC/NEDO.

JACKSON, M. (Ed.) (1989) 'Training Agency Waters Down YTS Requirement', *Times Educational Supplement*, 3 February.

JAMIESON, I. and LIGHTFOOT, M. (1981) 'Learning about Work', *Educational Analysis*, **2**, pp. 37–51.

JENKINS, R., BRYMAN, A., FORD, J., KEIL, T. and BEARDSWORTH, A. (1983) 'Information in the labour market: the impact of recession', *Sociology*, **17**, pp. 260–67.

JONES, B., *et al.* (1988) 'Finding a Post-16 Route', in Coles, B. (Ed.) *Young Careers*, Milton Keynes, Open University Press.

JONES, G. (1987) 'Young Workers in the Class Structure', *Work, Employment and Society*, **1**, 4, pp. 487–508.

JONES, G. and WALLACE, C. D. (1990) 'Beyond Individualisation', in Brown, P. and Chisholm, L. *Social Trends 18 and 19 (1988) and (1989)*.

KEEP, E. (1986) *Designing the Stable Door — a Study of how the Youth Training Scheme was Planned*, Warwick Papers in Industrial Relations, No. 8, Industrial Relations Research Unit, University of Warwick.

KELLY, J. R. and RAYMOND, L. C. P. (1988) *Leisure Activities of Unemployed Black and Hispanic Urban Youth*, University of Illinois at Urbana-Champaign.

KNASEL, E. G. and WATTS, A. G. (1987) 'Timing of employment selection within the Youth Training Scheme', *British Journal of Education and Work*, **1**, pp. 91–102.

KOSTERLITZ, J. (1985) 'Liberals and Conservatives Share Goals, Differ on Details of Work for Welfare', *National Journal*, 26 October.

LEE, D. (1989) 'The Transformation of Training and the Transformation of Work in Britain', in Wood, S. *The Transformation of Work*, London, Unwin Hyman.

LEE, D., MARSDEN, D., RICKMAN, P. and DUNCOMBE, J. (1990) *Scheming for Youth: A Study of YTS in the Enterprise Culture*, Milton Keynes, Open University Press.

LIVOCK, R. (1983) *Screening in the Recruitment of Young Workers*, Research Paper No. 41, London, Department of Employment.

LODZIAK, C. (1988) 'Dull Compulsion of the Economic: The Dominant Ideology and Social Reproduction, in *Radical Philosophy*, **49**, Summer.

MAAS, F. (1988) 'The abolition of junior unemployment costs — who should bear the costs' *Youth Studies Bulletin*, Vol. 6, No. 3, Australia.

MACDONALD, R. F. (1988a) *Schooling, Training, Working and Claiming: Youth and Unemployment in Local Rural Labour Markets*, unpublished PhD Thesis, University of York.

MACDONALD, R. F. (1988b) 'Out of Town, Out of Work: Research on the Post-16 Experience in Two Rural Areas', in Coles, B. (Ed.) *Young Careers*, Milton Keynes, Open University Press.

MCPHERSON, A. and WILLMS, J. D. (1987) 'Equalization and Improvement: Some Effects of Comprehensive Re-Organization in Scotland', *Sociology*, **21**, 4, pp. 509–39.

MARSDEN, D. (1986) *The End of Economic Man? Custom and Competition in Labour Markets*, Brighton, Wheatsheaf.

MARSDEN, D. and RYAN, P. (1988) 'Apprenticeship and labour market structure: UK youth employment and training in comparative context', paper submitted to international Symposium on innovations in Apprenticeship and Training, November, Paris, OECD.

MARSH, C. (1988) *Job Census in Chesterfield*, Manchester, BBC *Brass Tacks*.

MARTIN, J. and ROBERTS, C. (1984) *Women and Work: a Lifetime Perspective*, London, HMSO.

MAURICE, M., SELLIER, F. and SILVESTRE, J.-J. (1986) *The Social Foundation of Economic Power — a comparison of France and Germany*, trans. Goldhammer, A., Cambridge Massachusetts and London, MIT Press.

MSC/LAA POLICY GROUP (1986) *Work Related NAFE: A Guidance Handbook*, London, MSC.

MUNGHAM, G. and PEARSON, G. (Eds) (1976) *Working Class Youth Culture*, London, Routledge.

NATFHE (1984) *The Great Training Robbery: An Interim Report on the Role of Private Training Agencies within the YTS in Birmingham and the Solihull Area*, Birmingham, Birmingham Liaison Committee, Trade Union Resource Centre.

NATIONAL ECONOMIC DEVELOPMENT OFFICE (1988) *Young People and the Labour Market: A Challenge for the 1990s*, London, NEDO and Training Commission.

NEWMAN, C. (1989) *Young Runaways ... findings from Britain's first safe house*, London, The Children's Society.

O'MAHONY, B. (1988) *A Capital Offence: The Plight of Young Single Homeless in London*, London, Routledge.

ORGANISATION FOR ECONOMIC COOPERATION AND DEVELOPMENT (1985) *Education and Training After Basic Schooling*, Paris, OECD.

PAYNE, J. (1987) 'Does Unemployment Run in Families? Some Findings from the General Household Survey', *Sociology*, **21**, 2, pp. 199–214.

POLLARD, A., PURVIS, J. and WALFORD, G. (Eds) (1988) *Education, Training and the New Vocationalism*, Milton Keynes, Open University Press.

POLLERT, A. (1986) 'The Flexible Firm — Fixation or Fact?', *Work Employment and Society*, **2**, 3, pp. 281–316.

PRAIS, S. and WAGNER, K. (1983) 'Some practical aspects of human capital investment: training standards in five occupations in Britain and Germany', *National Institute Economic Review*, **105**, pp. 46–65.

PRESDEE, M. (1985) 'Agony and Ecstasy: Broken transition and the new social state of working-class youth in Australia' Occasional Papers No. 1, South Australian Centre for Youth Studies, Adelaide.

PRESDEE, M. (1987) 'Class, Culture and Crime and the New Social State of Australian Youth', paper presented to Australian Criminology Institute Biannual Conference, Canberra.

PRESDEE, M. and WHITE, R. (1987) 'Australian Youth Policies in the 80s', *Youth and Policy* No. 21, pp. 1–3.

PRESDEE, M. (1989) 'Made in Australia', in *Child Poverty and Australia*, London and Sydney, Allen & Unwin.

PRESDEE, M. (1990a) 'Creating Poverty and Creating Crime — Youth Politics in the 80s', in Taylor, J. (Ed.) *The Social Effects of Free Market Politics*, Hemel Hempstead, Harvester Press.

PRESDEE, M. (1990b) 'Knowing your place and the struggle for space', in Strockbridge and Turner (Eds) *Australian Youth Cultures*, London and Sydney, Allen & Unwin.

PROSSER, R. (1981) *The Leisure Systems of Advantaged Adolescents*, Unpublished PhD. Thesis, University of Birmingham.

RAFFE, D. (1983a) 'Some Recent Trends in Youth Unemployment in Scotland', *Scottish Educational Review*, **15**, 1, pp. 16–27.

RAFFE, D. (1983b) 'Employment Instability Among Less Qualified Young Workers', *British Journal of Guidance and Counselling*, **11**, 1, pp. 21–34.

RAFFE, D. (1984a) *Fourteen to Eighteen*, Aberdeen, Aberdeen University Press.

RAFFE, D. (1984b) 'The Transition From School to Work and the Recession: Evidence from the Scottish School Leavers Surveys', *British Journal of Sociology of Education*, **5**, 3, pp. 247–65.

RAFFE, D. (1984c) 'YOP and the Future of YTS', in Raffe, D. (Ed.) *Fourteen to Eighteen*, Aberdeen, Aberdeen University Press.

RAFFE, D. (1984d) 'The content and context of educational reform', in Raffe, D. (Ed.) *Fourteen to Eighteen: The Changing Pattern of Schooling in Scotland*, Aberdeen, Aberdeen University Press, pp. 214–30.

RAFFE, D. (1986) *The Context of the Youth Training Scheme: an analysis of its strategies and development*, CES Working Paper, No. 86/11, University of Edinburgh.

RAFFE, D. (1987a) 'Youth Unemployment in the United Kingdom 1979–1984', in Brown, P. and Ashton, D. N. (Eds) *Education, Unemployment and Labour Markets*, Basingstoke, Falmer Press.

RAFFE, D. (1987b) 'The Context of the Youth Training Scheme: an analysis of its strategy and development', *British Journal of Education and Work*, **1**, pp. 1–31; an updated version forthcoming in Gleeson, D. (Ed.) *Training and its Alternative*, Milton Keynes, Open University Press.

RAFFE, D. (Ed.) (1988a) *Education and the Youth Labour Market*, Basingstoke, Falmer Press.

RAFFE, D. (1988b) 'The Status of Vocational Education and Training 2: The Case of YTS', paper presented to the ESRC/DE Workshop on Research on Employment and Unemployment, London.

RAFFE, D. (1988c) 'Going with the grain: youth training in transition', in Brown, S. and Wake, R. (Eds) *Education in Transition*, Edinburgh, Scottish Council for Research in Education, pp. 110–23.

RAFFE, D. (1988d) 'Modules and the strategy of institutional versatility: the first two years of the 16-plus Action Plan in Scotland', in Raffe, D. (Ed.) *Education and the Youth Labour Market: Schooling and Scheming*, Basingstoke, Falmer Press, pp. 162–95.

RAFFE, D. and COURTNEY, G. (1988) '16–18 on Both Sides of the Border: A Comparison of Scotland, England and Wales', in Raffe, D. (Ed.) *Education and the Youth Labour Market*, Basingstoke, Falmer Press.

RAFFE, D. (1990) 'The Transition from YTS to Work: Content, Context and the External Labour Market', in this volume.

RANDALL, G. (1988) *No Way Home: homeless young people in London*, London, Centrepoint Soho.

REEDER, D. (1979) 'A recurring debate: Education and Industry', in Bernbaum, G. (Ed.) *Schooling in Decline*, London, Macmillan, pp. 115–48.

REES, T. L. and ATKINSON, P. (Eds) (1982) *Youth Unemployment and State Intervention*, London, Routledge & Kegan Paul.

REES, T. (1986) 'Education for Enterprise: The State and Alternative Employment for Young People', *Journal of Educational Policy*, 3, 1, pp. 9–22.

REUBENS, B. (1973) 'German Apprenticeship: Controversy and Reform', *Manpower*, US Department of Labour, 5, 11.

RIST, R. (1986) *Finding Work: Cross National Perspectives on Employment and Training*, Basingstoke, Falmer Press.

ROBERTS, K. *et al.* (1986) 'Firms' Uses of the Youth Training Scheme', *Policy Studies*, 6.

ROBERTS, K. (1987) 'ESRC Young People in Society/16–19: a sociological view of the issues', *Youth and Policy*, 22.

ROBERTS, K., DENCH, S. and RICHARDSON, D. (1987a) *The Changing Structure of the Youth Labour Market*, London, Department of Employment Research Paper No. 59.

ROBERTS, K., BRODIE, D. and DENCH, S. (1987b) 'Youth, unemployment and out-of-home recreation', *Society and Leisure*, 10, pp. 281–94.

ROBERTS, K. *et al.* (1988) 'Youth Unemployment in the 1980s', in Coles, B. (Ed.) *Young Careers*, Milton Keynes, Open University Press.

ROBERTS, K. and PARSELL, G. (1988a) 'Opportunity structures and career trajectories from age 16–19', Occasional Paper No. 1, ESRC 16–19 Initiative, Social Statistics Research Unit, City University.

ROBERTS, K. and PARSELL, G. (1988b) 'Life-style politics among Britain's 16–19 year olds', paper presented to *Economic and Social Research Council 16–19 Initiative Workshop*, Harrogate.

ROSIE, A. (1988) 'An Ethnographic Study of a YTS Course', in Pollard, A. *et al.* (Eds), *Education, Training and the New Vocationalism*, Milton Keynes, Open University Press.

RYAN, P. (1981) 'Segmentation, Duality and the Internal Labour Market', in Wilkinson, F. (Ed.) *Dynamics of Labour Market Segmentation*, New York, Academic Press.

RYRIE, A. C. (1983) *On Leaving School: A Study of Schooling, Guidance and Opportunity*, Edinburgh, Scottish Council for Research in Education.

SAKO, M. and DORE, R. (1987) 'How the Youth Training Scheme helps employers', *Employment Gazette*, June, 95, pp. 195–204.

SCOTTISH EDUCATION DEPARTMENT (1983) *16–18s in Scotland: An Action Plan*, Edinburgh, SED.

SEALE, C. (1985) 'Young People on the Youth Training Scheme in Further Education: A Survey of the First Year', *Educational Review*, 37, 3, pp. 241–50.

SHELDRAKE, J. and VICKERSTAFF, S. A. (1987) *The History of Industrial Training in Britain*, Aldershot, Gower Publishing Company.

SMITH, J. (1987) 'Women at play: gender, the life-cycle and leisure', in Horne, J., Jary, D. and Tomlinson, A. (Eds) *Sport, Leisure and Social Relations*, London, Routledge & Kegan Paul.

Social Trends, 18 and 19, London, HMSO.

SOLOMOS, J. (1988) *Black Youth, Racism and the State. The Politics of Ideology and Policy*, Cambridge, Cambridge University Press.

SPENCE, M. (1983) 'Job Market Signalling', *Quarterly Journal of Economics*, 97, pp. 355–74.

STAFFORD, A. (1981) 'Learning not to Labour', *Capital and Class*, **15**, pp. 55–77.

STEEDMAN, H. (1988) 'Vocational training in Britain and France: mechanical and electrical craftsmen', *National Institute Economic Review*, **126**, pp. 57–70.

STEWART, G. and STEWART, J. (1988) 'Forgetting Youth or how the state obstructs young people's independence', *Youth and Policy*, **25**, pp. 19–24.

STREEK, W., HILBERT, J., KEVELAER, K.-H., MAIER, F. and WEBER, H. (1987) *The Role of the Social Partners in vocational training and further training in the Federal Republic of Germany*, Berlin, European Centre for the Development of Vocational Training (CEDEFOP).

SUGARMAN, B. (1967) 'Involvement in youth culture, academic achievement and conformity in school', *British Journal of Sociology*, **18**, pp. 151–64.

Times Educational Supplement (1989a) 'Training Agency waters down YTS Requirement' (Edited by Mark Jackson), 3 February.

Times Educational Supplement (1989b) 'CBI advocates more power for Local Employers' (Edited by Mark Jackson), 21 July.

TRAINING AGENCY (1988) 'Skills supply and demand', *Labour Market Quarterly Report*, October, pp. 6–7.

TRAINING AGENCY (1989) *Enterprise in Higher Education: Key Features of the Enterprise in Higher Education Proposals, 1988–89*, Sheffield, Moorfoot.

TURBIN, J. (1988) *State Intervention into the Labour Market for Youth: the Implementation of the Youth Training Scheme in Three Local Labour Markets*, unpublished PhD, University of Leicester.

VOLZ, J. (1983) *Vocational Training and Job Creation Schemes in France*, Berlin, European Centre for the Development of Vocational Training (CEDEFOP).

WAGNER, K. (1986) *Relation between education, employment and productivity: a British-German Comparison*, Berlin, European Centre for the Development of Vocational Training (CEDEFOP).

WALLACE, C. (1987a) 'From generation to generation: the effects of employment and unemployment upon the domestic life cycle of young adults', in Brown, P. and Ashton, D. N. (Eds) *Education, Unemployment and Labour Markets*, Basingstoke, Falmer Press, pp. 108–37.

WALLACE, C. (1987b) *For Richer, For Poorer*, London, Tavistock.

WALLACE, C. (1988) *Youth and Policy*, **25**, pp. 25–36.

WALLACE, C. (forthcoming) *Youth in Society: Britain and West Germany compared*, London, Macmillan.

WARD, J. (1948) *Children out of School*, London, Central Advisory Council for Education.

WATTS, A. G. and MORAN, P. (Eds) *Education for Enterprise*, Cambridge, CRAC.

WESTWOOD, S. (1984) *All day every day: factory and family in the making of women's lives*, London, Pluto.

WHITE, M. (1988) 'Educational policy and economic goals', *Oxford Review of Economic Policy*, **4**, pp. 1–20.

WHITE PAPER (1981) *A New Training Initiative: A Programme for Action*, Cmnd. 8455, London, HMSO.

WHITE PAPER (1984) *Training for Jobs*, Cmnd. 9135, London, HMSO.

WHITE PAPER (1988a) *Training for Employment*, Cmnd. 316, London, HMSO.

WHITE PAPER (1988b) *Employment in the 1990s*, Cmnd. 540, London, HMSO.

WILLIS, P. (1985) *The Social Condition of Young People in Wolverhampton in 1984*, Wolverhampton Borough Council.

WILLIAMSON, H. (1982) 'Client Reponse to the Youth Opportunities Programme', in Rees, T. L. and Atkinson, P. (Eds) *Youth Unemployment and State Intervention*, London, Routledge & Kegan Paul.

WILSON, D. (1988) 'TVEI: The Agony and the Ecstasy', in Coles, B. (Ed.) *Young Careers*, Milton Keynes, Open University Press.

WOODS, P. (1983) *Sociology and the School: An Interactionist Viewpoint*, London, Routledge & Kegan Paul.

Notes on Contributors

Rosie Campbell is a Research Officer in the Department of Sociology at the University of Liverpool. She is presently working on a project which is examining participation in indoor sport in 6 UK cities. She is concerned with the changing nature of leisure services and the participation in sport by disadvantaged groups. Her writing interests have included leisure and sports policy. She has collaborated on an analysis of the Scottish Young People's Survey, examining the leisure behaviour of Scottish youth.

Joan Chandler is a lecturer in Sociology at South West College of Health Studies. Her research interests include the family, youth training and health. Her book *Wives without Husbands* is in the process of publication and she is presently researching mental health issues.

Bob Coles is a lecturer in Social Policy at the University of York. Throughout the 1980s he carried out research on post-16 progression in non-metropolitan, predominantly rural areas, some of which was reported in *Young Careers* (Open University Press, 1988), of which he was also editor. More recently he has worked on Equal Opportunities Policies and the work of the Careers Service and is currently carrying out research on youth training in rural areas.

Malcolm Cross is Principal Research Fellow at the centre for Research in Ethnic Relations. He has published a number of articles on youth and youth training and he has edited *Black Youth Futures* (1987). He has recently completed a study funded by the Department of Employment on the Careers Service and entry to the labour market (with John Wrench).

Andy Furlong worked as a Research Fellow at the Centre for Educational Sociology, University of Edinburgh since 1986 and is now lecturer in Sociology at the University of Strathclyde. He has published numerous articles on various aspects of the youth transition and the youth labour market and has co-authored a monograph of young people's routes into the labour market (with David Raffe).

David Lee is Senior Lecturer in Sociology at the University of Essex. He has written numerous articles on education, training and occupational stratification and is the author (with Howard Newby) of *The Problem of Sociology* (Hutchinson, 1983).

Mark Liddiard and Susan Hutson are researchers in the Department of Sociology and Anthropology at the University College of Swansea, specializing in issues concerned with young people. They have recently held a research contract with the Children's Society and carried out research for Barnardo's and National Children's Home. They are co-authors of *Street Children in Wales? A Study of Runaways and Homeless Young People in Four Counties of Wales* (The Children's Society, 1989).

Robert MacDonald has been researching youth culture, local labour markets and unemployment in the North of England for the past six years. His doctoral work focused on youth culture and transitions in predominantly rural areas. He is now Research Fellow in the School of Education, University of Durham and working on an ESRC 16–19 Initiative study of youth and the 'enterprise culture' in Cleveland.

Ken Parsons is a lecturer in Sociology at Worcester College. Since leaving school at 15 in 1969 he worked for ten years in a variety of jobs in industry. He read Sociology at York University, and studied for the PGCE at Huddersfield Polytechnic. His doctoral research is focused on the YTS in the South West. He was temporary lecturer at Polytechnic South West before entering his present post.

Mike Presdee lectured for fifteen years in Youth Studies and Sociology in South Australia. During this time he advised Ministers on Education and Youth policies and broadcast and published on these matters. He is now Senior Lecturer in Youth Studies at Christ Church College Canterbury.

David Raffe is Reader in Education and Co-Director of the Centre for Educational Sociology at the University of Edinburgh, where he has worked since 1975. His publications include *Reconstructions of Secondary Education* (with John Gray and Andrew McPherson, 1983), *Fourteen to Eighteen* (1984) and *Education and the Youth Labour Market* (1988). His current research interests include secondary and further education, the youth labour market, and education and training initiatives for the 14–18 age group.

Ken Roberts is Professor of Sociology and Head of Department at Liverpool University. His books include *Youth and Leisure* (Allen and Unwin, 1983) and *The Changing Structure of Youth Labour Markets* (Department of Employment, 1987). He is currently working on the Economic and Social Research Council's 16–19 Initiative, and on a study of indoor sports provisions and participants and the quality of life in six UK cities.

Claire Wallace is a lecturer in Applied Social Science at Lancaster University, having previously worked at Polytechnic South West. Her previous publications include *For Richer, For Poorer* (Tavistock, 1987) and *An Introduction to Sociology — Feminist Perspective* (with P. Abbott) (Routledge, 1990). She is currently researching into young people in the South West as part of the 16–19 Initiative.

Author Index

Abbott, P. 8
Ainley, P. 30, 76, 97, 112
Ashton, D. N. 23, 29, 30, 50, 53, 113, 114, 121
Atkinson, P. 30, 32, 34

Baddely, S. 34
Banks, M. H. 139
Barnett, S. 9
Bates, I. 29
Beardsworth, A. 55
Bedeman, T. 32
Bell, C. 71
Black, P. 38
Bland, R. 116
Boothby, J. 145
Brake, M. 1
Brodie, D. 134
Broomhead, S. 34, 35, 40
Brown, P. 5, 29, 30, 114
Bryman, A. 55
Bulmer, M. 2
Burghes, L. 13
Burnhill, P. 116
Burton, J. 14
Bynner, J. 52

Casey, B. 16
Chandler, E. J. 17
Chapman, P. J. 54
Chisholm, L. 5
Clark, J. 29
Cleveland County Council Careers Service 44
Cleveland County Council Research and
   Development Unit 43, 44

Clough, E. 52
Cockburn, C. 9, 24
Coffield, F. 50
Cohen, S. 1, 83
Cohen, P. 29
Cole, M. 79
Coleman, J. S. 135
Coles, B. 29, 50, 52
Collins, M. F. 145
Corney, M. 76
Courtenay, G. 32, 115
Cross, M. 5, 6, 97
Croxford, L. 130

Dale, R. 35, 97
Davies, B. 5, 76, 102
Deakin, B. M. 53, 62, 71
Dean, J. P. 75
Deem, R. 133
Dench, S. 50, 53, 62, 71, 134
Department of Education and Science 3
Department of Employment 31, 56
Department of Environment 172
Dodds, S. 130
Dombois, R. 11
Dore, R. 53
Dunnell, K. 143

Edwards, T. 74

Field, D. 113, 121
Finegold, D. 70
Finn, D. 24, 30, 46
Foord, J. 43, 46

Subject Index

Aboriginals 151
absenteeism *see* truancy
Afro-Caribbean 9 *see also* ethnic
apprentice/apprenticeship 15, 16, 99, 150
Approved Training Organization 34
Asian 9 *see also* ethnic
Australia 8, 146–63

Bed and Breakfast accommodation 166, 174, 178
benefits 5, 12, 52, 162–3, 178
biography 90, 130
black youth 2
Board and Lodgings regulations 7, 170, 175, 180
boys *see* males or gender
BTEC 3

Careers Service 21, 58, 176
Centre for Educational Sociology 2, 115, 129
Certificate of Education 90
Certificate of Pre-Vocational Education (CPVE) 3, 76
Chamber of Commerce 19
Charities 34
children/childhood 143, 145
Children's Society 164, 176
CITB *see* Construction Industry Training Board
City and Guilds 107, 109
City Technology Colleges 10
class 5 *see also* social division, working class and middle class
clerical work 63, 67
Cleveland County Council 43–51
client 166, 176
Clubs 131, 132

colleges 34, 77–8, 108, 39, 117, 151
Colleges of Further Education *see* colleges
Community Charge *see* Poll Tax
Community Programme 48
Community Service 99
Community Youth Support Service (CYSS) 156, 158
consciousness 79, 85
construction craft 67, 68
Construction Industry Training Board (CITB) 19
content of youth training 52–72
context of youth training 54–72
contract/agreement of training 17, 27
crime 8, 146–63
cultures *see* sub-cultures
curriculum 74, 94, 151, 152
CYSS *see* Community Youth Support Service

Department of Education and Science 3, 37
Department of Employment 17, 50
DES *see* Department of Education and Science
discourses 78–9
domestic work 132
domesticity 142–4
drugs 8, 154, 172
dual system 15

Economic and Social Research Council (ESRC) 2
education 136, 142
Education Reform Act 3, 10, 38
EHE *see* Enterprise in Higher Education
EITB *see* Engineering Industry Training Board
Employment Training (ET) 6, 14, 40, 45, 46, 47, 70

197